W9-CRX-112

LIGHTING GRANDMA'S

DATE DUE

DEDICATION

It's the rare person who accomplishes something without help or influence from someone important to him or the work. I am not the exception to the rule.

Stories that are successful in print or on film become so because they elicit a response from people. Some of the most memorable stories are those that leave us feeling warm and fuzzy: tales about happenstance and luck and happy relationships that make us wonder how things come about and just what is serendipity anyway . . . .

I don't have the answers. I just accept that, yes indeed, the experiences and relationships in my life have had a strong serving of serendipity and I am grateful for it. Without that magical force, I wouldn't have been exposed to the training I have had or learned the skills I've shared in this book. Nor would I have known Karen South Arnold. Without Karen and her fantastic work ethic, this book would likely never have been more than desultory conversation around a campfire. I dedicate it to her and to serendipity.

First Edition
Printed in the United States of America

ISBN 1-890437-33-6
Library of Congress Catalog Number 99-64981
Cover and text design by Laurie Goralka Design

Western Reflections Inc.
P.O. Box 710
Ouray, CO 81427

ACKNOWLEDGEMENTS

This kind of book doesn't just create itself from the mind of the author. No matter the amount of experience accumulated, the skills acquired, or the training involved, by the time the book is finished, it will have become a joint project.

I would never have thought to attempt this work except for the urging and support of two people: Dr. Karen South Arnold and Harry "Foxpaw" Carlson.

It took Harry at least a year of carping and cajoling to get this project started. His ability to see the world with eyes still open to wonder and a heart capable of purity is nothing short of miraculous. This old Massachusetts policeman knew it could be done and made a lot of suggestions that helped it along.

Dr. Arnold is solely responsible for all the wonderful graphics that illustrate these pages. Over many days and long hours, she cranked them out on her Macintosh computer (a machine of mysterious abilities). Her (intuitive, it seemed to me) sense of accuracy and eye for detail proved invaluable. When there were questions about historical data, she delved into her own extensive collection of books and spent considerable time in libraries to verify I was on the right track. Many of the chapters were her suggestions. Only an editor can truly appreciate Karen's unrelenting, tireless reading and rereading of the manuscript. Her peerless knowledge of English and its proper construction smoothed out what would have been many a glitch.

I am also indebted to that consummate artisan and mountain man, George S. Knowlden, for his willingness to share details of how he builds lazybacks. I appreciate too the time George spent in reviewing the raw manuscript. He's a busy man. Once you learn to recognize his work, you will see it all across this nation; after you've seen it once, you'll never mistake it. It is so popular, in fact, that much of it has been stolen.

The things I have shared here I didn't learn all on my own. I have had numerous mentors in my life, just one of whom is Warren "Hawk" Boughton of Kentucky. I owe all of them, wherever they are today, much. And I would be remiss if I failed to acknowledge that very important classroom where I first learned many things that helped me in my life: the "rocky mountain college" of the American Mountain Men.

To all of you I tip my hat and say from my heart, thank you, I am indebted to each of you.

Bill Cunningham
Colorado 1999

FOREWORD

The mountain men of early America were required, by their very isolation from "civilization," to have a wide variety of skills and knowledge just to survive. Many who followed those early trailblazers—pioneers, cowboys, Army scouts—used some of the same skills, but over time much of their knowledge fell into disuse and was forgotten.

Modern tools, technology, and materials have made yesteryear's skills obsolete. Or have they? Outdoorsmen wearing clothing made of modern synthetics have died of exposure where pioneers clad in wool or leather survived handily. People stranded or lost have starved or been immobilized because they lacked fundamental survival skills that every child of earlier generations grew up with. If the electrical power goes out, today's households may lack heat, light, or entertainment. Yesterday's homes got along quite well without our modern amenities.

Mountain men spent months, even years, in the wilderness with not much more than flint and steel, knife, hatchet, and flintlock rifle as basic equipment; they came home fit and fat. By contrast, campers and hikers today finance a multi-billion dollar industry to support their weekend forays. Stoves, sleeping bags, and tents that weigh mere ounces and are designed to withstand the worst nature can throw at them are common. Alloy-frame backpacks, aluminum (once the world's most expensive metal) mess kits, prepared foods, tiny propane lanterns, breathable waterproof boots with lug soles, and water filters that can process sewer water into sweet nectar are a must. Still some get lost, become injured, starve, die.

Historical reenactors and survivalists have developed an abiding interest in doing things without the benefit of today's technology and cost. Judged by current standards, some of their exploits using only historical equipment and skills are truly amazing. Much of the equipment they use cannot be purchased. It must be made. Through research and trial and error, they have learned what the mountain men knew.

Various basics are here: how to light a fire with flint and steel, make rawhide or tan a small fur, build a pair of snowshoes, fashion a hat that will protect you from the elements, build a pair of leather pants, or sew together a pair of moccasins.

It is fun and educational to learn and use the skills that were common in our history. We are reminded of a simpler time when the day seemed to have more hours in it, and people took the time to help neighbors build a cabin or barn. Do we want to return to those days? Probably not. But the knowledge and perspectives we gain from them can benefit us today and, in certain circumstances, even save our lives.

TABLE OF CONTENTS

MAKING
A SLOUCH
HAT

MAKING A SLOUCH HAT

Hats are such a personal item that finding just the right one may be difficult. Purchasing a slouch hat can be tough because those low-crowned, flat-brimmed beauties are usually all of one style. And that often is just not quite what you want. A good one is expensive, and the price is enough that you don't feel comfortable with the idea of customizing it. That's understandable. There is a way, however, to overcome this problem: make your own – not from scratch, but from a castaway.

MATERIALS

To make the slouch hat, you will need:

> Hat (see selecting a hat)
> Artificial sinew (recommended) or crochet thread
> Needles for sewing
> Soft leather for hatband
> Thong for stampede strap
> Beads or other decoration (optional)

SELECTING A HAT

The first step is to find a suitable candidate. Thrift stores, going-out-of-business sales, yard sales, swap meets, and rummage sales are all good sources. Because the prices of old hats usually are low (25 cents to $5.00) and don't discriminate between felts made of fur or wool, you may as well go for the superior fur (preferably beaver) felt.

"Beaver felt" itself is a misnomer. On the inside band, you will often find a number of Xs. Three Xs indicate that the hat is made of 20 percent beaver and 80 percent rabbit fur. Five Xs indicate 30 percent to 35 percent beaver, while seven Xs tell you that the hat contains 40 percent to 45 percent beaver, and so on. The more beaver fur, the better the felt. For your purposes, anything from a three-X up will do. There are some older hats that are of excellent quality that are not marked; in those cases, go by the brand name.

Because of the wide brim, old (or new) western ("cowboy") hats offer the best possibilities for making a slouch hat, but there are certain criteria they must meet. They should be made of good fur felt, although if you are especially taken by one that is of wool felt, you *can* make it do. They don't need to be stain-free unless you're finicky about such things. Holes in the crown are a "no-no" and the flat-top variety is not as good for making slouch hats as the domed styles. Also beware of hats with radically sloped or shaped crowns. You want a hat that will provide a round dome with even proportions. Poke the crown up and note the shape of it.

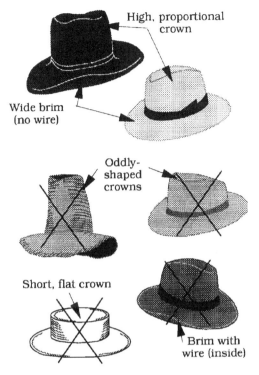

High, proportional crown

Wide brim (no wire)

Oddly-shaped crowns

Short, flat crown

Brim with wire (inside)

Once you've located a candidate – feel it, look it over for excessive wear, heft it and judge if it is of a weight you will enjoy wearing. Try it on to see how it feels.

The hat should fit a little loosely –
as much as a quarter size too large

A hat that does fit just right can work, but the amount you can modify it will be less.

Be sure you like the color. "Wear" marks (usually on the top of the crown) can be removed with fine to medium sandpaper to blend them into the surrounding area.

Look at the inner band to see how many Xs are stamped on it.

The lining (presence, absence, poor quality) doesn't matter.

But the sweatband *is* important. Pick a hat that has a sweatband made of leather, not plastic or cardboard.

Check out the brim. It has to be wide enough to suit your preferences.

Avoid a hat that has a wire sewed inside the outer edge of the brim to help it keep its shape. The wire is usually there because the material in the hat is not good enough to hold a shape on its own. In general, that hat will not be one that will do the job for you.

Once you've found the hat that is just right, pay for it and take it home. Before you become too enamored of the hat to ever change it, tear out the liner (if it has one), remove any hatband, and throw them away.

PREPARING THE HAT

Set a teakettle of water to boiling. Place the hat upside down in a bucket. The edge of the bucket should support the brim and keep the hat from sliding down inside. Pour the boiling water slowly through the hat, being sure to wet all the crown. Use all the water; the purpose is to wash out every bit of the stiffener put in by the manufacturer so it would hold its shape.

When the crown has cooled enough to touch, push all the shape out of it with your hand, leaving it domed much like the one Hoss Cartwright wore on *Bonanza*. If the hat has a curled brim, heat another kettle of water and pour it on until the brim will lie flat. Set the hat aside, right side up, on a flat surface and let it dry.

CUTTING THE HAT

When the hat has dried to the touch on the outside, it is ready for the next step. Make a mark on the inside center front of the crown — extend it from the stitching down inside the sweatband to at least halfway up the crown. Continue the mark outside the sweatband onto the brim for about 1 inch.

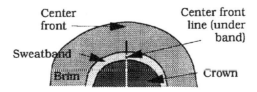

Center front

Center front line (under band)

Sweatband

Brim

Crown

Pulling the sweatband down out of the way, draw a line around the inside of the crown just above one-half the width of the sweatband up from the stitching. Take a sharp cutting tool, such as a razor blade, and cut the crown off along the line. *Don't cut the sweatband,* only the crown. Be sure you cut in a level, straight line to prevent having to work on a varying surface later.

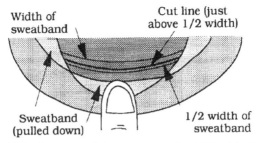

Width of sweatband

Cut line (just above 1/2 width)

Sweatband (pulled down)

1/2 width of sweatband

Cut 1/2 inch off the bottom of the crown and set it inside the brim to determine how low the crown has to be to suit your taste. When you have it just right, note how much horizontal gap is between the crown and the upper edge of the felt above the brim. You are going to have to sew the crown back on, and it will only stretch so much. If there is much more than a 1/4-inch gap all the way around, you ought to reconsider what looks "just right." If the crown is still too tall (the bottom edge is below the edge of the brim), take a soft lead pencil or a scribe and make a line all the way around the crown opposite the upturned edge of the brim.

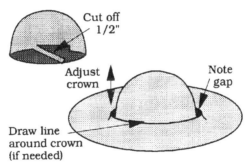

Cut off 1/2"

Adjust crown

Note gap

Draw line around crown (if needed)

Remove the crown and cut off the material below the line if you drew one (it shouldn't be much). Make sure you remove an equal amount all the way around.

SEWING THE HAT

Get out your sewing equipment. If you are using artificial sinew (recommended), split it into thirds. Otherwise, use something soft, such as a double strand of crochet thread that is the color of the hat. Turn the sweatband down out of the way. Match up the marks you made to locate front and center on the brim and crown. Abut the brim and crown and secure the brim to the crown with a couple of tack stitches at the center front. Next take tack stitches *exactly* opposite at the center back. Then tack both sides halfway between front and back to divide the hat into quadrants.

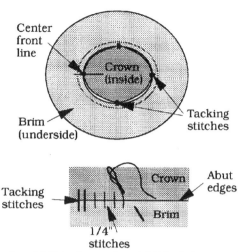

Center front line

Brim (underside)

Crown (inside)

Tacking stitches

Tacking stitches

Crown

Brim

Abut edges

1/4" stitches

Make stitches, about 1/8 inch apart and 1/4 inch long, to join the crown to the brim. Pull each stitch firmly enough that the felt edges come together securely, but not so much that it puckers. If you are experienced at sewing, you can make stitches that do not show on the outside. That is neat, but if your work is more of the gross order, go ahead and push the needle clear through, up and over each side. It won't show on the finished product. Sew one quadrant at a time. To prevent puckering or migration of "gap," once one quadrant is finished, switch to the opposite one and do it next.

When the crown is totally secured to the brim, try the hat on to be sure it fits the way you want it to. One that is a little too tight will not stay on in the wind. If you have taken off a significant amount from the crown, the size will have changed. If it has, wet the entire crown (including the sewed surfaces) and the inner 2 inches of the brim. Put the hat on, pulling it down tightly. Wear it around until it is dry. This may sound stupid, but a short while in the sun or the warming influence of a hair dryer will do the trick. The felt will stretch to fit unless you've cut off a truly huge amount of the crown. Should that be the case, using your new expertise, go out and find another suitable hat in a larger size and start over.

SETTING THE SHAPE

Mix a cup of sugar with a quart of boiling water and stir the mixture until all the sugar is dissolved. If you are not a total historical purist or don't like bees buzzing around your head all that much, get a can of spray starch instead. Find a location where over-spray is not going to be a problem. Smooth the hat into the exact shape you prefer. If you are using sugar water, it can be applied with a brush or a spray bottle. Whichever stiffener you choose, really wet the hat with it. When it has dried, it will hold its shape, but there will probably be little "sparkles" all over it. Without too much elbow grease, use a medium-soft brush to take them off.

FINISHING THE HAT

Assuming that all has gone well, it is time to cover the evidence of your modifications. Select a nice piece of brain- or garment-tanned leather 3/4 inch wide and a little longer than enough to reach completely around the bottom of the crown. This will be your new hatband. If you don't have any leather, stores such as Tandy do or you might find a worn-out leather jacket for a buck at a thrift store. Take some bacon grease and wood ashes (or any suitable substitute – don't use the one that occurs to you when you've been up too late) and rub the mixture into one side of the leather strip. *Don't use a petroleum-based oil!* It will seep through and "bleed" out into the felt. Give the band some time to dry, anywhere from an hour to a day, depending on the leather and climate.

With the clean side to the felt, sew the band onto the hat. If you are using sinew, split it at least into thirds, preferably fourths. If not, use a single strand of button-twist thread. Make tiny stitches on the outside, spacing them up to 1/4 inch on the inside. Stitch both top and bottom edges of the band to within 1 inch of each end. Pull each stitch tight, but not tight enough to pucker. Be careful that the band will join ends at the exact rear of the hat. Sew the joining edges at the rear of the hat by turning the edges under 1/8 inch (trim off excess) and doing hidden stitches. Finish sewing the upper and lower edges of the hatband to the hat. Press the joint flat at the back of the hat with a moderately warm iron. If it makes too much of a bulge for your taste, cut the ends so they abut and sew them to the felt with tiny stitches.

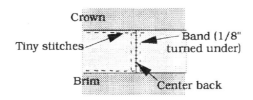

PERSONALIZING THE HAT

You can add some of your own touches such as a quilled or beaded hatband, but it should go over, not replace, the leather hatband.

By sewing a small patch, open at the ends, at a slight angle on the side of the hatband before attaching the band to the hat, you will have a dandy place to thread a turkey feather or badge decoration.

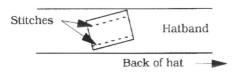

Another option is to add a stampede strap to keep your hat on in the wind. A strap, such as one of braided horsehair, may be purchased or you may make one of many materials, such as boot laces. It may be adorned with beads, bones, silver doodads, and other items. There are also many ways to attach the strap to the hat; two are suggested here.

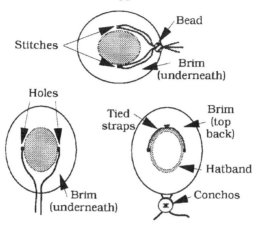

The simplest way is to sew the strap to the brim underneath and about halfway from front to back. A second choice is to punch holes in the same location, thread the straps through to the top of the brim, and tie the two ends together at the back of the hat.

To keep the straps together and allow a snug adjustment to the back of your head, thread them through a bead or animal vertebra. Two conchos, concave sides together, also work well.

You now have a very personalized slouch hat of high quality that, if you were judicious in your shopping, cost you less than five bucks and a couple hours labor. Wear it proudly!

MAKING LEATHER TROUSERS

MAKING LEATHER TROUSERS

There are many reasons for making leather trousers: historical reenacting and practicality are most common. The reenactor of certain historical time periods almost *requires* leather trousers. The outdoorsman, horseman, and sports enthusiast often can *benefit* from them.

Pants made of a good grade of garment-tanned leather or of brain-tanned leather will long outlast fabric under nearly any conditions. They provide protection against thorns and brush, rock and sand, and insect bites.

Contrary to a popular misconception, because they breathe, they are cool in hot weather and warm in cold. There are many who claim that the more stained and use-worn leather pants become, the more attractive they are.

For the reenactor, old paintings (by artists contemporary to the time period of interest) and many costume books provide significant details of line and construction. Patterns for trousers, both historical and modern, abound. But following a commercial pattern puts a lot of complications into what can be a pretty simple project. These instructions can be used by either school. The historical buff can make a few modifications and comply with period clothing's line and fit.

The time required for making leather trousers will depend on your tenacity and ability. For the novice who also has to work for a living, plan on a couple of hours an evening for most of a week. Trousers *can* be finished in just a couple of evenings or one precious day out of a weekend.

TOOLS AND MATERIALS

To make a pair of leather pants, you will need:

A pair of scissors (not the best pair in the house lest the purported owner get bent)
A couple of needles (curved veterinary needles work especially well)

Artificial sinew (unwaxed dental floss makes a decent substitute)
A sharp blade or seam ripper
A soft lead pencil
Leather (below)
Strips of material for "stiffener" (such as light- to mid-weight horsehair canvas)
Buttons [purchased, deer antler (p. 25), etc.]

If you aren't comfortable freehanding stitches, leather-working supply shops sell a handy little tool to make holes for perfectly spaced stitches. You will need a small hammer or mallet to strike the tool.

3 to 6
teeth

If you are using factory garment-tanned leather, it should be a light tan color – not bright yellow or orangish. If you order by mail, be very specific about this. It should be deer or garment-tanned cowhide. *Do not use splits – they are too thin for rugged use!* You can use elk, but it is heavy.

The amount you need will be determined by your size. Once you have prepared your pattern, you will have a better idea, but in general you will require 21 to 28 square feet, contained in one or two hides. That represents a significant outlay of cash and it is wise to shop around for quality and price. The suppliers listed in the back of the book have been tried and found reasonable.

PREPARING THE PATTERN

In lieu of a conventional pattern, you will need an old pair of pants that fits the way you prefer. Patches or holes don't matter (in fact, the more worn, the better, because you will destroy the pants. You are going to cut them into either two or four pieces, depending on whether or not you want an inside leg seam (inseam).

There are two schools of thought about inseams. With an inseam, you have more control of your work (but a little more sewing). Also making the trousers flare at the ankle is easier.

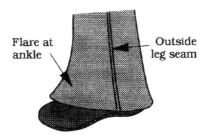

Flare at
ankle

Outside
leg seam

Horsemen often claim that legs without inseams make for more comfortable riding – a subjective statement, but one with popular credence.

Pants made without an inseam require less sewing, of course, but also demand that you take extra care in sewing exactly the same size stitches on the *outside* leg seam. To keep it from "migrating" around behind the leg when you are finished, each stitch must be pulled with *exactly* the same pressure as the last.

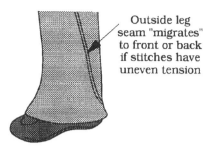

Outside leg seam "migrates" to front or back if stitches have uneven tension

Regardless of which style you prefer, the basics are the same.

Before you cut your old trousers to make a pattern, draw a line across both legs on the wrong side just below where the fly ends. Start on one leg and go clear across to the other.

If the material is dark, use sharp chalk or even a running stitch of bright thread. The line will be an anchor point when you begin to sew later. Also on the inside, mark pants' pieces for left and right, back and front, such as LF, RB. A piece of masking tape on each section works well for dark colors.

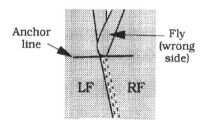

Anchor line

Fly (wrong side)

LF   RF

Now cut the old trousers to make your pattern. Pants with flat-felled seams (like Levi's) should be cut up the middle of the seam. For other types of seams, rip the stitching, being careful not to tear the fabric, and trim the edges to 1/4 inch outside the old seam line. Cut the outside leg seams and the center back seam all the way around the crotch just to the fly stitching. At that point, cut a small notch in the right front to free the fly, then cut through the zipper. To make pants with an inseam, cut the pattern pants' inseam in addition; for leather pants with no inseam, leave the pattern inseam intact.

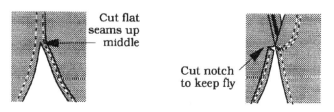

Cut flat seams up middle

Cut notch to keep fly

Using a hot iron, press the liberated seams flat. Remove all buttons and mark clearly where they were.

PREPARING THE LEATHER

Stretch, lay out, and cut your trousers in one time period.
If you do not, relationships of the pieces can change
as the leather shrinks back.

If you have someone around to help, have him grab one end of the leather while you get a firm grip on the other. Stretch it for all you're worth: first across the grain (width), then with the grain (length). If you are by yourself, do the best you can. It's fair (and effective) to use knees and elbows in your effort.

LAYING OUT THE PATTERN

You will need a large work surface. The floor does just fine, but if it is carpeted be careful when cutting that you don't cut more than you intended.

Decide whether you want the smooth or rough (suede) side out. If you keep the smooth side to the inside, it is easier to see what you are doing, and most people prefer the fit, action, and look of trousers made this way. Whichever you choose, take special care when cutting that all pieces are cut to the same side of the leather.

Assuming that, like most folks, you want the rough side out, lay the rough side face down on your work surface. If you are on a carpeted floor, lay something like newspaper, a drop cloth, or cardboard down first. If you don't you will eventually find that you've created a vacuum cleaner nightmare that will take major effort to clean up.

Lay the pattern pieces, right side down, on the smooth side of the leather (see Layouts, **Figures 1–4**). (All right. If you insist on making pants with the smooth side outside, just reverse things here.) Place pieces *with the grain* (lengthwise) so subsequent stretch will be lengthwise. Placing them diagonally or across the grain will create bagginess and a tendency for seams to migrate. The stretch will recover in odd ways.

Adjust the pattern pieces until you have achieved optimum use of the leather. Be sure no holes line up on the pattern edges. In the interior, don't worry about holes that are the size of a half-dollar or less. Avoid holes larger than this if you possibly can. *Don't worry either that the fronts are shorter than the backs at the waist; don't lengthen the fronts to match the backs – it's that way to give you bun space!*

Once you have the leather and pattern adjusted, be sure there are no wrinkles underneath. Using your pencil, draw a line on the leather, outlining the pattern. On all pieces, extend the lines above the waistband another 3 inches (or less if you don't have enough leather). On LF, block out either an additional 6 inches for a diagonal fly or 3 inches for a button-front fly. On RF add 2 inches along the fly for an overlap. On all pieces, extend the legs 1 inch if there is enough leather.

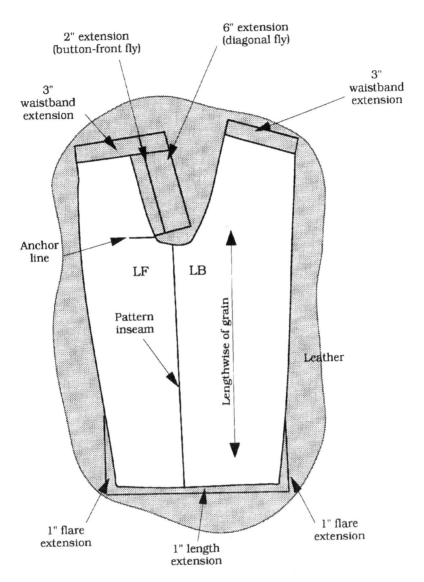

2" extension
(button-front fly)

6" extension
(diagonal fly)

3"
waistband
extension

3"
waistband
extension

Anchor
line

LF

LB

Pattern
inseam

Lengthwise of grain

Leather

1" flare
extension

1" flare
extension

1" length
extension

Figure 1. Layout for Trousers Without an Inseam (left leg)

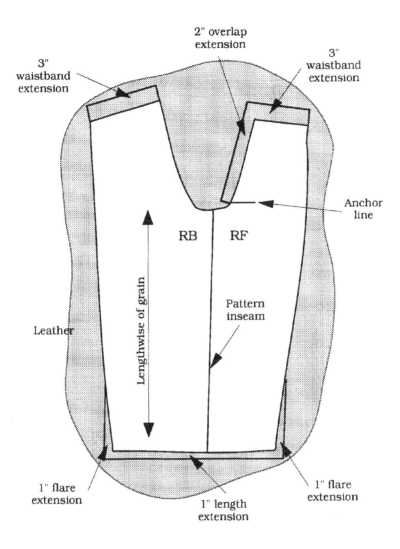

Figure 2. Layout for Trousers Without an Inseam (right leg)

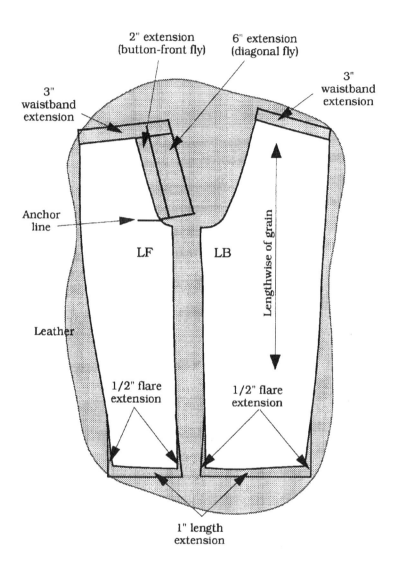

Figure 3. Layout for Trousers With an Inseam (left leg)

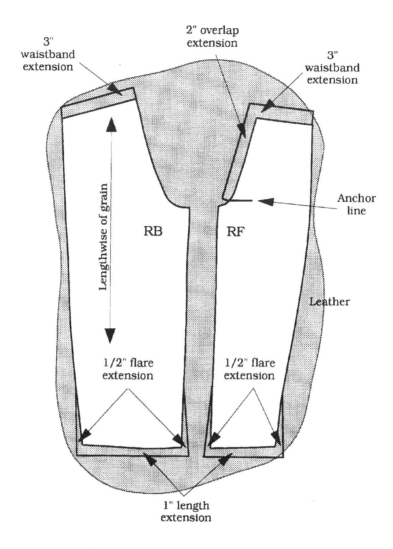

Figure 4. Layout for Trousers With an Inseam (right leg)

A little flare at the ankles makes pants easier to put on and is helpful in keeping water out of your footgear if you get wet. To do this, stand flat-footed on a firm surface and measure up to where you want the flare to start (usually at the top of the ankle). For pants with an inseam, extend the leg width 1/2 inch on either side at the bottom and taper the line to the measured spot above. If you've chosen a pair of trousers without an inseam, add 1 inch to each outside edge. Eventually it will fall right, especially after you get it wet.

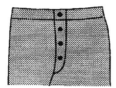 

Button-front fly   Diagonal fly

Before removing the pattern pieces, mark each leather piece with the identifying letters you made on the patterns (LF, RF, LB, RB). Being very accurate, draw an anchor line on the leather below the fly *exactly* where you made the line on the pattern.

CUTTING THE LEATHER

The Mystic Moment or Doing the Deed

You have reached the moment of total commitment. It can be positively mystic! Don't let it throw you. Double-check that the pattern outlines make a left and a right leg relative to the proper outside surface, the fly extensions are defined on the proper leg, the flares are drawn in, and the waist is extended. Now go ahead and cut. Do it as neatly and straight as you can, but don't worry too much about minor variations. Leather is forgiving!

Cut welting strips from scraps. If you want fringe on outside leg seams, cut strips about 6 inches wide; the length of *each* strip doesn't matter, but you need a *total* length equal to that of both seams. If you don't want fringe, cut pieces the same length, but only 1/2 inch wide. In addition, cut 1/2-inch-wide welting strips with a total length equal to that of the butt seam around the crotch to the fly plus the inseams (if you have them).

If you use the stitch spacing tool, make holes 1/4 inch in from the edge around all seam edges, 1/4 inch in from cut edge of fringe welting, and down the middle of 1/2-inch welting.

SEWING THE TROUSER SEAMS

All seams will be sewn with the right sides together (wrong side facing you). *Use welting between the two pants' layers for all seams.* For fringe on outside leg seams, it is preferable to put the rough side toward the front of the pants and *remember – the fringe welting will be between the layers of pants so it will be on the outside when you turn them right side out.*

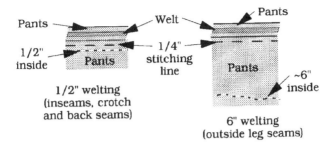

1/2" welting
(inseams, crotch
and back seams)

6" welting
(outside leg seams)

Keep the edge of the welting even with the top edges of the seam; use a running stitch. If you have not made holes with the tool, keep the stitches no longer than 1/4 inch; 1/8 inch is better if you have the patience. Every 3 to 4 inches, go back through the last stitch to lock stitching firmly.

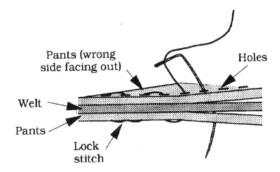

If you are using sinew, split it at least in half, preferably thirds. You have to use dental floss as it comes from the spool. For those creative souls who want to buck-stitch with leather strips instead of sewing – you're on your own!

Sewing the seams in a specific order and direction (**Figures 5 or 6**) prevents spacing problems. It also helps to prevent slippage if you line up each seam and tack or pin the pieces together in several places along the length before you begin to sew.

Turn your trousers right side out. Admire what you have accomplished so far.

SEWING THE FLY

Follow the instructions below for the type of fly you have chosen (diagonal fly, button-front fly with exposed or unexposed buttons).

Diagonal Fly. Fold under the 6-inch leather block on a diagonal from the crotch toward the right hip until you achieve the "look" you want. Make sure

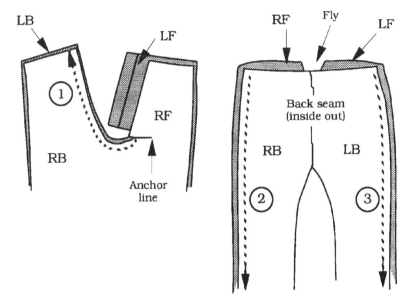

Figure 5. Seam Order and Direction for Sewing Trousers Without an Inseam

① Sew crotch and back seam from anchor line to waistband at back.
② Sew right outside leg seam from waistband to pants bottom
③ Sew left outside leg seam from waistband to pants bottom.

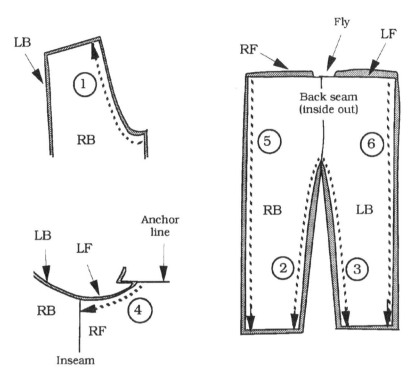

Figure 6. Seam Order and Direction for Sewing Trousers
With an Inseam

①   Sew center back seam from edge to waistband.

② ③   Sew right leg inseam from crotch to leg bottom, then left
      leg inseam from crotch to bottom.

④   Sew remainder of crotch seam from anchor line to
      inseams.

⑤ ⑥   Sew right leg outside seam from waistband to bottom,
      then left leg outside seam from waistband to bottom.

the overlap is at least 2 inches along the fold from top to bottom. Trim off excess to 2 inches.

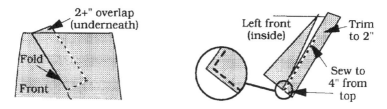

Cut a 2-inch strip of stiffener (horsehair canvas), if you want to use it to prevent stretching, and place it inside the folded-over fly up against the fold. With running stitches, sew the fly to the pants across the bottom and the inside raw edge to within 4 inches of the top. The right front fly for diagonal-fly pants needs no further work. Go to waistband instructions.

Button-front fly (exposed buttons). A button-fly front can be done with buttons exposed or unexposed. For exposed buttons, fold the left fly flap to the inside (2 inches wide). Insert a 2-inch piece of horsehair canvas (if desired) and place it inside against the fold. Sew the edge down with running stitches, catching the pants front only about halfway through the leather (stitches do not show on the right side). Go to right front fly instructions.

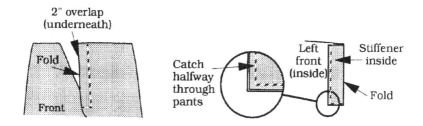

Button-front fly (unexposed buttons). Measure from the anchor line above the crotch to the top of the front. Cut a 4-inch-wide piece of leather the length of your measurement to make a placket. Fold it in half, right side out, and insert a 2-inch piece of stiffener (if you want it) inside, up against the fold. Trim off the 2-inch block you added to the left fly.

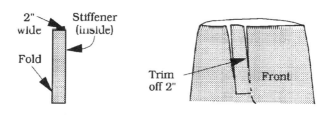

On the inside, align the folded edge of the placket with the left front edge of the pants. Sew the placket on the inside along the bottom and the side away from the opening. Catch the pants front only about halfway through the leather (stitches do not show on the right side). Stop sewing 4 inches from the top of the pants.

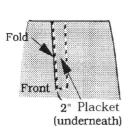

Fold

Front

2" Placket
(underneath)

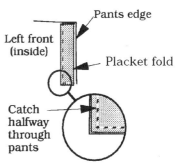

Pants edge

Left front
(inside)

Placket fold

Catch
halfway
through
pants

Right front fly. For button-fly pants, cut a piece of stiffener 1 inch wide (if you want it). Fold the fly extension so 1 inch is to the inside and put the stiffener inside to the fold. Sew the fly to the inside of the pants with running stitches as before.

WAISTBAND

Try the trousers on again and pin them in place. Pull and tug at the trousers until they fit in the crotch and seat just the way you want them to. If the seat is baggy, make marks where it needs to be taken in, tear out your stitches, and redo it. The overall fit may be snug. Unless you are trying for a casual, baggy look, snug is good. The leather will stretch and mold to your shape as you wear the pants so you can make a fine figure of a man! If the legs hang a little long, stand on a firm surface and have someone else mark the length you want them to be. Don't cut them yet.

Fold the excess leather on the waistline down inside the pants until the top is where you want the pants to hang. Mark the fold line (the leather's, not yours) with a pencil. If the piece inside is less than 2 inches, trim the waist edge to your pencil mark and forget the folded waist. It will work, though it may stretch with time. (Inside the waist, you may also want to sew on a 2-inch-wide strip with stiffener to prevent stretching.)

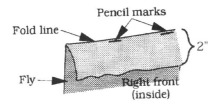

Pencil marks

Fold line

2"

Fly

Right front
(inside)

If there are 2 or more inches of leather folded inside, trim off any excess to make the folded-over band 2 inches wide. Cut a piece of stiffener 2 inches wide and the length around the top of the pants. Put it inside up against the fold of the band. Sew the band to the pants, using the same size stitches as before and catching the pants only halfway through the leather.

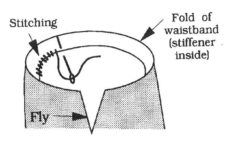

To eliminate bulk, the right fly for either button-front and the left fly with exposed buttons should be trimmed before you sew down the ends of the band:

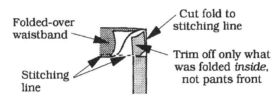

For a left button-front fly with unexposed buttons, just cut off both layers of the *placket only*. Because the left front of the pants is not a folded edge, there is no need to cut along it to the stitching line as above.

For a diagonal left fly, trim as follows:

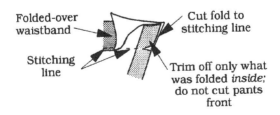

For the diagonal fly, the waistband itself should be squared off at the point it meets the fly.

To finish the waistband, sew the ends over the right and left fly. Sew together each end of the band.

FINISHING THE TROUSERS

Buttonholes. Mark the left fly where you want the buttonholes. Center one vertically in the waistband and space the others evenly for the length of the fly. With a sharp blade, slit your marks the length of the diameter of your buttons. *Remember for a button fly with unexposed buttons cut through the placket only; do not cut the front of the pants.*

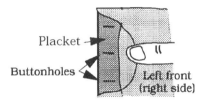

Placket →

Buttonholes <

Left front
(right side)

Sew *tiny* overlap stitches around the buttonholes through all thicknesses.

Buttons. You can use any buttons that appeal to you: wood, shell, deer antler, etc. If you prefer antler, take a branch of a size that appeals to you (a diameter of 3/4 inch to 1 inch seems in favor, but smaller can work) and, with a hacksaw, cut the number of slices (about 1/8-inch thick) you need. With a file or wire brush, remove burrs, then drill two small holes opposite each other, one on each side of center.

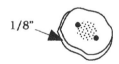

1/8"

If you wish (and it is wise to do so), smooth the sides and round off sharp edges with a file or grinding wheel. If you plan to wear suspenders with your trousers, make some smaller buttons of a size that will easily go through the buttonholes of the suspenders.

Sew the buttons to the trousers with sinew split in half or with dental floss. It is recommended that you do not sew suspender buttons on until you have the suspenders available so you can locate the buttons in the right places. Try the buttons in the holes. If they are too large or too small, make new ones of the correct size.

Belt Loops. From the remaining scraps, cut four to six pieces of leather 4 inches wide and 3/4 inch longer than the width of the belt you will use. Lay a piece of stiffener on top of each. Double them lengthwise and sew the sides together.

Seam

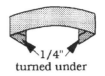

1/4"
turned under

Fold under 1/4 inch on the ends of each loop and sew them to the trousers, spacing them evenly. Placement will depend on the type of fly you have, but putting a loop any farther than 4 inches out from left center front may mean you have difficulty getting the end of your belt to reach.

Leg Length. Put the pants on and get them adjusted so they fit just right. Are the legs still too long? Re-mark them if necessary. They should be just to the ground in back (but don't cut them higher in the front). Once you mark them, cut them 1/2 inch longer initially if you have the leather. The first time they get wet, they will dry to fit right, unless you get wet to the knees — then they'll stretch to fit a pro basketball player. But don't worry, they'll retract when they dry and can be trimmed again if it is needed.

Dealing with Those Holes. Garment-tanned leather, especially deer and elk, often comes with holes. You can patch them in several ways. For delicate work like patching, a small needle (glover's needle) works well.

One way is to trim any really ragged edges. Lay the hole over a piece of scrap leather and draw an outline of the hole on it. Cut out the drawn patch. Place it in the hole, matching the shape. Sew it in using the same stitch you would to sew moccasin soles — go in halfway through the edge of the leather of the patch, come out above on the wrong side, loop the stitch over the edge and go in again halfway on the edge of the pants. Bring the exposed part of the stitch out on the inside of the trousers. The stitches won't show on the outside of the pants and, with a little rubbing or wear, will be all but invisible.

Edges of leather

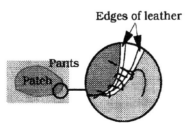

Pants

Patch

Another method of fixing holes, if they are not overly large, is to turn the pants wrong side out and fold the leather across the hole so its edges come together. Using as little seam allowance as possible, sew the edges tightly together. When you turn the pants right side out, the repair can hardly be seen.

Edges of leather — — Stitches

The third method is to catch the edges of the leather without bringing the stitching out to either side. This requires a very small needle, fine thread, and good eyesight! When you finish the hole, pull the thread tight, pulling the edges together, but not tight enough to pucker the leather. You may not be able to see the repair, and only you know it's there!

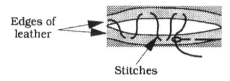

Edges of leather

Stitches

Fringe. If your welting on the outside leg seam was made wide enough for fringe, lay the pants and welting flat on a table. Trim the top welting flush with the pants (see below) for about 4 inches (mid-hip or to your taste) and, at the bottom, angle the cut down. The fringe begins below this point from here, cut the welting into strips, the narrower the better (e.g., 1/8 inch). As you cut, angle the strips down to make the fringe longer.

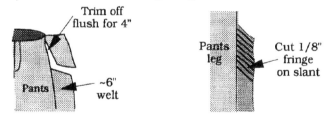

Finally, trim the welting flush with the pants on all unfringed seams.

Wear your new trousers with pride!

FROM THE GROUND UP: MAKING INDIAN MOCCASINS

FROM THE GROUND UP:
MAKING INDIAN MOCCASINS

There are nearly as many styles of Indian moccasins as there are tribes. These instructions are for "plains" style footwear. Except for minor details that identify one tribe from another, they are typical of many of those worn historically from the Missouri River to the Sierra Nevada mountains.

MATERIALS

The leather you choose for the top part may be factory-tanned or brain-tanned; it may be deer, elk, moose, or cow. Thinner leather is more desirable than thicker leather and, if they are good quality, splits will work.

Leather for the soles is a different matter. You can make soles from the same leather as the tops, but they won't last very long. Rawhide is all right if you only walk on dry ground but, if you get it wet, it will stretch and give you a lot of problems. Well-tanned, thick leather, such as latigo leather, is best and is easy to obtain.

It is wise to make a pattern from paper or poster board before you buy your leather. That way you can measure the amount of each kind of leather you will need to make your moccasins.

Having said all that, the materials you will need are as follows:

Glover's needle (size 11 or 12) or veterinary needle

Leather for the tops
Latigo leather for the soles
Paper or poster board for a pattern
String
Artificial sinew or buttonhole twist thread
Three-cornered awl

MAKING PATTERNS

To draw your patterns, be sure to *sit* when you trace your foot or tie the string. Standing increases the size of your feet, and the moccasins are going to stretch as you wear them. Sitting will create a smaller shoe that will remain more snug with time.

Making the sole patterns. First put your feet on your pattern material. With a soft-lead pencil, draw a line around each foot. Leave some room between the tracings and be sure to hold the pencil straight up and down so the lead doesn't slip beneath any part of your foot. (Some people make a pattern of one foot only and reverse it for the other foot, but feet are rarely the same size.) Draw a line 1/4 inch wider all the way around for a seam allowance.

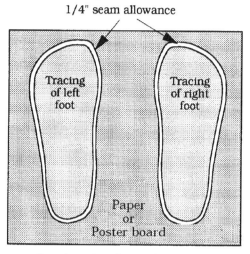

Next, with your pencil and a ruler, draw a line across the widest part of each foot (seam allowances included) — line X-Y extended through allowances **(Figure 1)**. Draw a second line (line A-B) lengthwise, perpendicular to and centered on line X-Y.

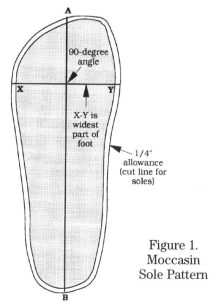

Figure 1.
Moccasin
Sole Pattern

Now wrap a string around the widest part of one foot and tie the ends snugly. Slip the string off your foot and cut it next to the knot. Lay the string on the width line (line X-Y) for the proper foot pattern and cut off a piece 1/2 inch shorter than the distance between X and Y (**Figure 1**). Throw it away. The remaining string is the width of the top of the moccasin including a 1/4-inch seam allowance on both sides. Repeat the string instructions for the other foot.

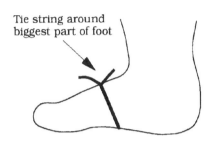

Tie string around biggest part of foot

Cut out the sole pieces following the seam allowance lines of your foot patterns.

Making the top patterns. Place the sole patterns on top of the paper or poster board. Make sure you have a left and a right foot. Also make sure you have enough paper to add 1/2 inch to the top of each toe and 1/2 inch to the bottom of each heel.

Draw around the sole patterns and mark the paper at the ends of line X-Y and line A-B. Remove the sole patterns and connect the marks to make the intersecting lines. Extend the line A-B 1/2 inch at toes and 1/2 inch at heels. Extend line X-Y (equally on both sides of line A-B) to equal the length of the string; this makes line X'-Y' in **Figure 2.**

Draw the tops, starting at the center front (1/2 inch above sole pattern) and making curved lines to the widest part of the foot (X' and Y'). Extend the lines from X' and Y' straight to 1/2 inch beyond the heel. Square off the heel ends, making line Q-R (which is 1/2 inch longer than the sole pattern). Line Q-R equals the length of line X'-Y'. Finally draw a line from the midpoint of line Q-R to the midpoint of line X'-Y' (line O-P). This completes **Figure 3.**

Cut out the patterns (**Figure 3**). Cut along line O-P from heel to line X'-Y'. Cut perpendicular to line O-P (along X'-Y') for 1 inch to each side.

Except for leather for tongue pieces and thongs (ties), you now know how much leather you need. For rough figuring, add two pieces 4 inches wide and 6 inches long (to make tongues) and one piece about 6 inches square (to make ties).

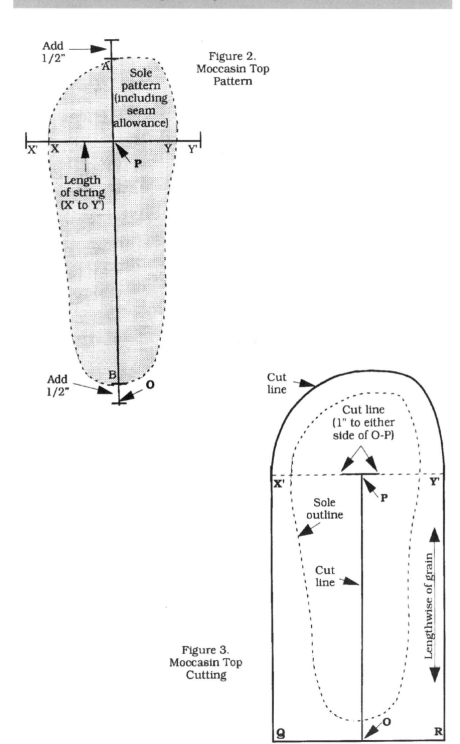

Add 1/2"

Figure 2.
Moccasin Top Pattern

Sole pattern (including seam allowance)

X' X Y Y'

Length of string (X' to Y')

P

Add 1/2" B O

Cut line

Cut line (1" to either side of O-P)

X' Y'

P

Sole outline

Cut line

Lengthwise of grain

Figure 3.
Moccasin Top Cutting

Q O R

CUTTING THE MOCCASINS

Lay the sole patterns on the sole leather with the smooth side of the leather down. Trace them with a pencil *(never ink!)*, mark each L (left) or R (right), and cut them out.

Now place the top patterns on the top leather. Place them to conserve leather, *but do not place them on the bias;* trace them so the rough (or suede) side will be the outside of the finished moccasin. Mark the line O-P from the center of the heel to line X'-Y' and the 1 inch cuts along line X'-Y'. Mark the tops L or R and cut them out. Cut line O-P from the heel and the lines to 1 inch on either side of O-P.

SEWING THE MOCCASINS

Before you begin sewing, especially if you use a glover's needle, you may want to make a leather "thimble" to protect your thumb and aid pushing the needle through the leather layers. Cut a piece of heavy leather about 4 inches long and 1 inch wide. At one end cut a hole that will slip over your thumb snugly. To use the thimble, slide the hole over your thumb and down to its base; flip the other end up to cover the pad of your thumb.

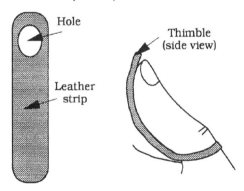

Hole

Thimble
(side view)

Leather
strip

Sewing is best done with artificial sinew or with a strong thread, such as buttonhole twist. If you use sinew, split the strands into thirds. The glover's needles or veterinary needles have three-sided points to make holes that will not tear or stretch.

From your scraps of soft top leather, cut welting strips about 1/2 inch wide (they can be any length).

You will assemble the moccasin wrong side out — the smooth side of the sole and the rough (suede) side of the tops go against each other. The seams should have a strip of welting between the sole and the tops along the edge. Use a "whip stitch." Push the needle through the tops, the welting, and slant it to come out the *side* of the soles. Make the stitches 1/8 inch apart.

Sewing the toes. It is a good idea to clamp the heel of the tops to the heel of their soles, overlapping the back edge of the heel 1/4 inch beyond the lengthwise line on the sole (for sewing the heel seam later). It is also very useful to divide the distance from the toe to the heel into thirds or fourths and clamp or tack the sole to the tops at those points to hold the leather from moving as you sew.

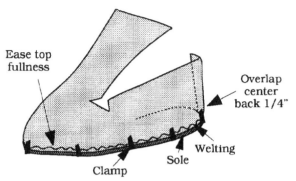

Start sewing at the center of the toe and move along the side toward the heel (**Figure 4**). Make the stitches about 1/8 inch apart and use a 1/4-inch seam allowance. Slant the stitches so you come out through the *side* of the sole. Pay close attention to what the top leather is doing as you sew. Because the tops are larger than the soles, you must take up a little of the top fullness with each stitch. It's what gives you "toe room" when the moccasin is finished, and it should be spread evenly in very small puckers along the seam. Don't pucker the welting.

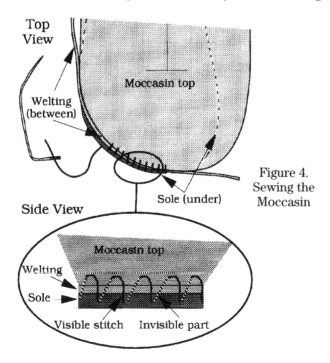

Figure 4.
Sewing the
Moccasin

When you finish sewing the first side, go back to the toe, place your clamps and welting along the other side (overlapping the heel 1/4 inch beyond the line), and, beginning at the toe, sew the other side (**Figure 4**).

Sewing the heels. The heel can be sewn in one of two ways; both use an in-and-out running stitch that is back-stitched in several places to lock the seam. The leather will tend to splay out at the top of the heel; take care to keep the seam at a 90-degree angle to the sole.

One way is to put a piece of welting between the backs of the heels, abutting the heel ends and turning the seam to the inside (when finished). The other, which makes a flatter seam, is to just overlap the 1/4-inch allowance, without using welting, and sew a flat rectangle.

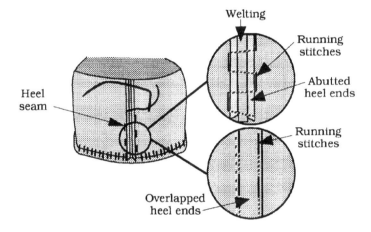

If you desire, you may stitch a patch of soft leather around the inside (or outside, if you prefer) of the heels to stiffen them. If you don't want the patch to show, put it on the finished inside (the side facing out since your shoe is still inside out). Trim welting (if you used it) close to the stitching before you sew the patch. Sew the patch on with small stitches (either whip stitches or running stitches) that do not go completely through to the right side.

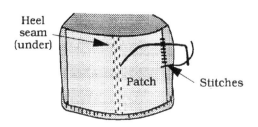

Sewing the tongues. Turn the moccasins right side out and try them on. Enlarge the 1-inch cuts evenly from the center cut if it is necessary to make the moccasins comfortable. Be careful not to make them *too* comfortable; you want them snug because they will stretch with use.

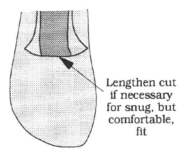

Lengthen cut
if necessary
for snug, but
comfortable,
fit

Make tongues from the soft leather, each 2 inches wider than the cut and 6 inches long. You may cut a large notch in one end (decoration). Place the tongues on the outside of the shoes, centered on the cut, rough side down, and decorative notches (if you cut them) toward the heels. Using welting, sew the tongues to the tops of the moccasins.

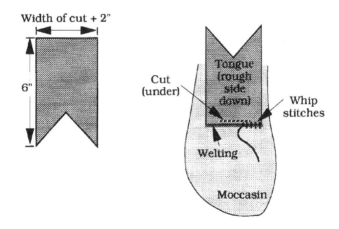

Width of cut + 2"

6"

Cut
(under)

Tongue
(rough
side
down)

Whip
stitches

Welting

Moccasin

FINISHING THE MOCCASINS

With a three-cornered awl or glover's needle, make evenly spaced holes around the moccasins about 1/2 inch from the top edge. A little planning helps here. It is good to have the lacing on the *outside* across the back of the heel, so that's a good place to start. The lacing weaves in and out. On the outside it can be as long as 1 to 1 1/2 inches; underneath it should be about 1/2 inch. Also make holes in the tongue in a rectangular pattern.

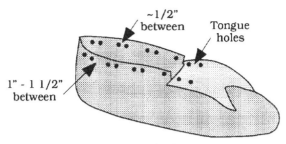

Cut two leather thongs from the soft leather. One way to get nice, long thongs is to cut them from a 6-inch circle. Cut the thongs about 36 inches long (trim later if needed) and 1/4- to 3/8-inch wide in a continuous circle:

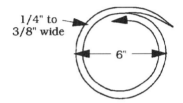

Thread the thongs through the holes. Put the moccasins on and tie the strings on the front so they hold the folded-over tongues in place.

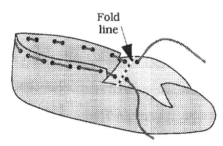

The last step is to trim the welting from around the sole so it is flush with the seams. Though stitches do not show, be careful not to trim so closely that you cut any stitching.

Happy hiking!

ADDENDUM:
ADDING HIGH TOPS TO YOUR MOCCASINS

It's easy to make higher tops on your moccasins if you want them. They can be added to any desired height.

For each moccasin, cut a piece of soft leather to the following dimensions:

Length (L): 1 1/2 times the circumference of your leg at the
    thickest place your tops will cover

Height (H): The distance from the top of the moccasin to the highest point on your leg you want the tops to reach

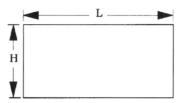

Right side facing out, center a high-top on the outside of the back seam of each moccasin; overlap it 1/4 inch. Put welting between the moccasin top and the high-top and sew the addition on the moccasin using running stitches (**Figure 5**).

Figure 5. Sewing High-Tops onto Moccasins

You will need a second set of laces to wrap the high-tops. Cut them at least 3/8 inch wide as before and long enough to wrap around your leg several times to the top of the high-tops. Tie them into the holes next to the tongue.

When you wear them, wrap the flap on the outside of the leg to the inside and the inside flap over it to the outside of your leg. Holding them in place, wrap the new thongs around your leg to the top and tie them off.

FIRE KITS
AND
STARTING
A FIRE
WITH FLINT
AND STEEL

FIRE KITS AND STARTING A FIRE WITH FLINT AND STEEL

Flint-and-steel firemaking has benefits beyond doing something *historical.* It is an efficient method of starting a fire that sometimes outperforms modern means, such as matches or lighters. Flint and steel will often start a fire on those wet, blustery days when a match needs a pint of gasoline to get a blaze going. A flint-and-steel fire kit need not be bulky and it does not add significant weight to a pack. Kept in a small metal box, it can be forgotten until it is needed.

Flint-and-steel kits have several components: a container, usually a metal box with or without hinges; a striker; a piece of flint; char; and tinder.

CONTAINERS

Whitman Sampler or cough drop boxes; old flat, round, film canisters; or the old Edgeworth pipe tobacco boxes work well. Unwanted paint can be removed by placing the box in a hot fire, waiting for the paint to burn off, then scrubbing the box with a wire brush.

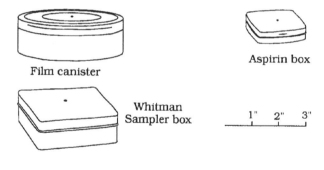

Film canister

Aspirin box

Whitman
Sampler box

1" 2" 3"

STRIKERS

Iron strikers come in various styles and sizes:

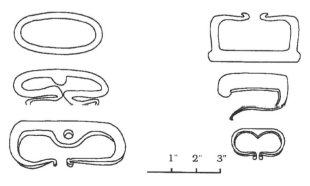

1" 2" 3"

FLINT

Flint is a bit of a misnomer, as many rocks that are not technically flint can be used. Anything that is hard enough to shave tiny bits of metal from the striker in the form of sparks will do. Many people constantly try their strikers against rocks that have caught their eye. Sometimes they replace the one in their fire kit with the new find (keeping the old one just in case). Keep in mind that whichever piece of stone you choose, it should be shaped so that it has one or more sharp edges and fairly flat surfaces so that it can be held firmly; it should be of a size that will fit into your fire kit container.

CHAR

Although other materials, such as some woods or plants, *can* be used, char is commonly a *cloth* that has been carbonized. The cloth must not have been treated with a fire retardant. Unbleached muslin works very well as does untreated linen or cotton, although finding untreated cotton can become a career. Untreated muslin and linen don't cost all *that* much and can be purchased in most fabric stores. Old diapers or tee-shirts, no matter how worn or aged are not good candidates. That fire retardant really lasts through the best detergents and harshest washing cycles. Char made from treated cloth may *look* good, but it will not catch and hold a spark reliably.

To turn cloth to char, cut it to fit the metal box you have chosen to hold your fire kit. Using whatever tool you have handy (a finish nail will do), poke a small hole in the top of the box. Fill the box full of cloth pieces. Close the box tightly and place it on the coals of a hot fire. You also may use the burner of a propane camp stove or even the kitchen range (though you might set off the smoke alarms). The box will not admit enough air for flame, but the cloth will slowly turn to char. As it does so, smoke or a small flame will appear from the hole you poked in the top of the can. The smoke or flame will burn for as long as there are materials to dissipate from your cloth.

Once the smoke or flame disappears, you can remove the can from the coals. (Be careful not to allow it to open, such as by dropping it. If you do, a big glowing coal that was your cloth – and should have been your char – will drop out and it's all over). Most people let the can stay in the fire for a few more minutes just to be sure. This isn't necessary, but tends to make them feel better until they discover that they've overcooked things and the char is too brittle.

Once the can has become cool enough to touch, you may open it and inspect char of your own making. The cloth will have shrunk to about half its original size and, of course, its color will have changed. Dull dark black is good. You may even see the weave of the material. Pick up a piece and tear it into two pieces. It should be fragile, but handleable. The torn edges should be ragged and may have tiny pieces (threads) showing. If the material is shiny black and is brittle and breaks or shatters, start over – you used a synthetic cloth. If the material has a brown tinge to it and is soft-looking, you probably used a treated cloth – start over.

TINDER

Tinder comes in many forms. Types and availability depend on where you are geographically. In the East, dry cedar bark, roughed up between the palms of your hands, is excellent, much like the bark of the ubiquitous juniper (often called "cedar") in the West. Most any bark that is dry and can be abused into a dusty, stringy "bird's nest" will work. Of course, a real bird's nest (preferably without the birds or eggs) is a real winner. Dry grass will work, but so much of it that looks dry will prove to contain moisture and won't burn. Combed flax or unraveled sisal rope is often carried as tinder. They work well, but are hygroscopic; that is, if it is raining, or even very humid, they will collect moisture. If this has happened, even though they may appear dry, they will smoke like crazy, but will not burst into flame. Good material can often be found under old deadfalls, in the crevices of rock fences and cliffs, or animal dens. Practice makes for proficiency. Go forth!

MAKING FIRE

Now that you have flint, steel, char, and tinder, you are ready to practice. Whether you merely want to see if you can get the char to catch or go all the way to a fire, the basics are the same.

First, get all your materials ready. If you want flame, get a fire pit arranged and collect wood, from dry twigs to wrist-size pieces. Form some tinder into a circular "bird's nest" about the diameter of a coffee cup and as thick as your wrist (approximately 3 to 4 inches diameter by 2 to 3 inches thick) and place it within easy reach.

Tear a piece of char into two pieces. Pick up your flint and hold it between the thumb and forefinger of your left hand, sharp edge toward you. (All right, lefties, hold it with your right hand and do everything the opposite from what is explained here.) Be sure the flint protrudes at least slightly beyond the knuckles beneath your forefinger. The first time you don't, your scraped flesh will tell you why! Put a piece of char between your thumb and the flint, ragged edge toward and nearly even with the sharp edge of the flint.

Taking the striker in your right hand, strike the flint a glancing blow. Do this in an arcing motion, flexing your wrist to help accomplish it. This is important. It's the same motion a guitar player uses to strum with a "loose" wrist. By using an arc, you bring the striker *away* from your knuckles. You also drag more of the metal surface across the flint, which literally shaves pieces from the steel and makes sparks which, hopefully, are caught and fostered by the char (the ragged edge helps facilitate this) and the char will start to burn.

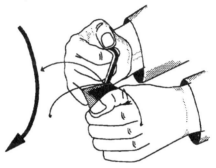

If at first you don't succeed and are too impatient to practice, you can try placing the char on your knee and striking sparks from above it. Another trick is to wrap the char completely around the flint, giving you two surfaces in which the spark can catch.

When you have "caught" a spark, place the char in the center of the tinder (or bird's nest) and fold the tinder material, completely but gently covering the char. Hold the tinder in front of your mouth (not too close — you don't need to kiss it!) Purse your lips and blow semi-vigorously into the bird's nest in the area where you placed the char.

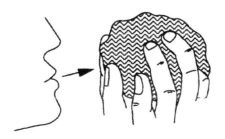

Smoke will billow, and soon flame will flash suddenly over the rear surface of the nest. (It can be disconcerting, especially if you have a cupped death grip on the tinder or sport a dry, fluffy beard.) Stop blowing and place the flaming bundle into your fire pit. Starting with the smallest twigs, feed your fire until it takes larger wood.

Another way to start your fire is to place a piece of "gathered-up" glowing char against the wick of a candle (in front or behind) and blow until you see a blue flame. Stop blowing instantly. You will have a lit candle.

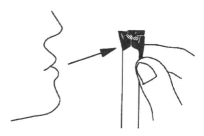

If this doesn't work for you, expose more of the wick, wrap the top inch of the candle and the wick with char, place the glowing char against it, and blow. The wrapped char will also catch and eventually so will the wick. You will be left with a messy, blackened candle, but you'll have flame to start a fire.

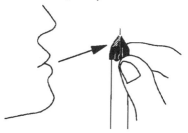

STORAGE

Now that you've proven your system, you need to put it away, ready for use when you need it. The spare tinder, if you have some, can be carried in a pouch, a can, or even your pocket. The container you burn char in can carry all the other items. First put in your char. Next, cut a piece of leather the size of the interior of the can and put it on top of the char to protect it. Now put in your flint with the striker on top of it. Some people put it all in an old aspirin can. If you've properly sized everything, it will be crowded, but will fit. Close the can.

If you want to waterproof your can, rub a wax candle around the joining surfaces and over the vent hole until it is sealed. You may even, should you choose, light the candle and drip wax around and over things until you are satisfied. Either way, the interior goods will remain dry even in a hurricane.

DUTCH
OVEN CARE
AND
FEEDING

DUTCH OVEN CARE AND FEEDING

As popular as Dutch ovens are today, it's easy to forget just how far back they go historically. The ovens probably were not invented by the Dutch. But traders from Holland sold or traded so many of them, especially to the Indians and early settlers in America, that the ovens acquired the name.

Dutch ovens were manufactured in early New England as well. Paul Revere, in fact, made many, improved on the originals and, except for the detachable handle he put on some, today's models are near-copies of his. Of all the equipment Lewis and Clark took along on their journey to the Pacific, the two things they refused to give up to the Indians were their guns and the large Dutch oven they carried. John Colter, who became one of the most famous of Lewis and Clark's crew, owned one. When he died in 1813, his estate was auctioned off. Among the things listed was a Dutch oven that went to John Simpson for $4, the equivalent of a week's pay.

There are some very good reasons for owning a Dutch oven. Not only do they produce great outdoor meals with a minimum of fuss, but they also can be just as handy at home. They are great on the coals of an open fire or in a pit dug in the ground, but they perform superbly on a stove burner or in a conventional oven. Once set up, they cook fantastic meals and turn out beautiful bread, biscuits, pies, and cakes. The minimal attention they require during cooking makes them seem almost magical.

A plethora of cast-iron cooking implements have been developed since Paul Revere was handcrafting Dutch ovens. Oblong cast-iron cookers, round kettles with flat bottoms, and frying pans with lids are not the real article. These may all work well, but they are made for kitchen cooking. Cast iron alone does not make a Dutch oven — the design is critical!

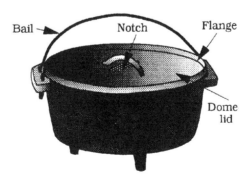

A true Dutch oven is heavy, with thick walls and a flat bottom that has three legs about 2 inches long spaced to form a tripod. The kettle has a bail. The lid is also heavy iron and fits tightly. It has a slight dome to it and a cast handle in the center that is too squat to get your fingers under comfortably. Beneath the handle (on truly good, older ones), there is usually a small notch. It's a balance point for picking up the lid with a hook. The edge of the lid has a flange to facilitate holding hot coals. Be sure the one you get has a lid that is round and not warped.

Dutch ovens are available at many sporting goods stores. They often can be found in good used condition at secondhand stores, garage sales, and swap meets. Once you begin using a Dutch oven, something happens that you didn't foresee. You get better at cooking with it and, to expand your abilities, you buy another and sometimes even a third one. They come in various sizes, generally from 8 to 16 inches in diameter. If you are going to own only one, the 14-inch size is probably the most versatile.

CLEANING AND CONDITIONING YOUR OVEN

Well, first things first. New, used, or off a scrap pile, your Dutch oven needs to be cleaned and seasoned before it can be used. New ones have a fine wax coating to protect them; it has to go. The steps for preparing any oven are as follows:

1. If your oven is coated with rust, it must be removed. Do not attack it with a Brillo pad, a wire brush, or ScotchBrites. They will draw any seasoning out of the iron. Don't use solvents or chemicals — cast iron is porous (that's why it works so well) and it will absorb the stuff and later come back to haunt you. The best way to remove rust is to heat the Dutch oven, melt lard or heat oil in it, then take a rough cloth (burlap is good) and wipe the rust until it is gone. If you use soap, use non-detergent (Ivory works well).

2. Heat the oven until it is warm to the touch but not hot enough to burn your hand. Using hot water and *non-detergent* dish soap, wash the oven and the lid thoroughly.

3. Rinse and heat them until they are dry.

4. To season the oven, put some vegetable oil, lard, or Crisco in it and heat until the lard is melted or the oil is good and warm. Spread it over the walls and bottom of your oven, including the inside of the lid. Heat the lid and oven until the oil smokes. The heating process opens the pores of the cast iron so the oil can penetrate (see box below).

5. Let the oven cool, then wipe off the oil until there is just a thin film left. If you leave too much on it, the oil can turn rancid.

6. Put the lid on the oven and set it aside until you want to use it. At that time, if there is rust, repeat step 1. If you use soap, the oven will have to be reseasoned.

If you want to *really* season your oven, put it on a stove at the lowest possible heat and fill it up to the top with oil, lard, or Crisco. Put the lid on and leave it alone, but keep an eye on it. As it processes, you may need to add oil to replace what is absorbed by the iron and bring the level back to the top of the oven. When you see the outside glisten, it's done. This can take up to three days or more. The oil will have turned black and cannot be reused for cooking, but it makes great waterproofing for winter moccasins, boots, or other leather items. Of course every neighborhood dog and cat is likely to follow you around for awhile . . . .

There are a couple of other cleaning methods in use out there. *They are not recommended!* You may have seen people clean out the inside of a Dutch oven by putting it upside down over a campfire. Don't be tempted. Burning it out can damage the metal and in other ways cause you a lot of extra work. To prevent further rust, the oven will have to be reseasoned right away. The other method "cleans" the oven without washing it. People scrape the inside free of debris with a putty knife or spatula, then wipe it out with a cloth. Though the seasoning remains, it gives bad germs a medium to grow in.

COOKING WITH YOUR DUTCH OVEN

Your Dutch oven is a versatile vessel designed to cook delicious food. It will bake, broil, roast, fry, or stew. Outdoors the kettle may be hung from a tripod over the fire, set on the coals of a small fire, or buried in a pit. It can be left unattended while the meal cooks. All that's required is knowledge of how to set up the oven for each cooking method and the amount of time each will take. Above-ground cooking is the fastest because the fire is hotter. Pit cooking is slower and can take from 4 to 8 hours for roasting or stewing.

Dry hardwood is the preferred fuel because it makes hot, long-lasting coals. Even in the Rocky Mountains, where the primary growth is soft wood, hardwood often can be found among the scrub growth of oak, maple, dead box elder, and even dead alder or mountain mahogany. The goal is not enough wood for a blazing inferno — just enough coals to cook dinner.

Two small fires are very useful for cooking above ground. One is for cooking on and the other is to supply additional coals, especially if you are using soft wood that will be quickly consumed. Distribute the coals for the cooking fire so they form a flat bed. You want the oven and its contents to be level. Be sure the bed of coals is spread enough to extend slightly beyond the oven so that the heat will be even. *Never, never set the kettle only partially onto coals – uneven heat can warp or even crack the metal.* Take coals from the second fire and scatter them over the lid. You don't have to smother it — an evenly spaced dozen or so walnut-sized coals will do. Depending on the quality of your wood, you may have to replenish the coals occasionally until the meal is cooked. When you do, be sure they provide a level surface for the oven.

Some people prefer charcoal briquettes to firewood. Go easy with them. They are generally larger than wood coals and burn hotter. For 14- to 16-inch ovens, about eighteen coals evenly spaced beneath the oven and a dozen on top are plenty.

If you want to be away from camp all day, yet have a main dish ready when you return, the pit method of cooking works wonderfully. (It's not a good idea for baking because cooking time for pastries and biscuits is relatively short.) First dig a hole about 4 inches larger (all the way around) than the circumference of your kettle. Line the hole with rocks, but *do not* use those from a streambed; they can explode from the moisture content within them. You can dispense with the rocks, but getting rid of dirt that adheres to the pot is more work than lining the pit. At least line the bottom of the hole; it works better than just dirt. Build a fire in the pit and keep it going for about an hour or long enough to heat the stones thoroughly.

Prepare the food and put it in the oven while the fire is burning down to a level bed of coals. Put the lid on and give it a little turn to ensure it is securely in place. When the coals are ready, remove enough of them to cover the entire lid. Set the Dutch oven in the pit, make sure it is level, and cover the lid with coals. Refill the hole, covering the lid with about 4 inches of dirt. Go away. A roast or stew will be cooked in about 4 hours, but still hot and ready to eat in 8.

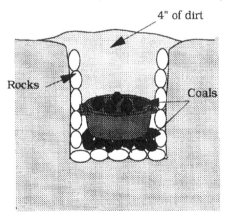

4" of dirt

Rocks

Coals

You can prepare food in two or more Dutch ovens at the same time and stack them. Each successive one takes heat from the coals on the lid of the one below.

Whenever you remove your cooking from the fire and it's ready to serve, remove the lid so condensed moisture doesn't drip into the food.

For all Dutch oven cooking, certain tools are useful: shovels, a piece of stout cloth like burlap for cleaning and as a pad to keep your hands from being burned, and one or more hooks. A variety of shovels can be used for digging holes and moving coals. Burlap bags, available at feed or specialty stores, will last a long time as pot holders and dishcloths. Hooks are more personal; they can be obtained from a variety of sources and many tools intended for other uses can be adapted. Blacksmiths often make pot hooks at reasonable prices. A pry or wrecking bar can be adapted, as can a claw hammer with an extended handle.

Hook   Pry bar   Tree limb

DO'S AND DON'TS FOR DUTCH OVENS

Do heat the oven until fat melts (or heat oil well); then sear all meat before cooking it to keep the juices in.

Do warm the oven a little before putting anything in it.

Don't use the fat of wild animals (except bears) to grease or season your oven.

Don't ever, ever pour cold water into a warm oven; it may cause the metal to crack.

Don't loan your oven to *anyone* unless you are prepared to lose it, to have it ruined, or to go through the cleaning and seasoning process as soon as you get it back.

SOME DUTCH OVEN RECIPES

Now that you have a clean, seasoned oven and have learned the fundamentals of cooking, it's time to actually try something. The recipes presented here are very basic and used at some time or other by just about every Dutch oven cook. They will get you started. To broaden your repertoire, most bookstores have good books, usually small and inexpensive, on Dutch oven cooking. With experience, you may discover, however, that you stick to basics and modify them as your taste and imagination dictate.

Beef Pot Roast

This is a pretty standard item to cook in a Dutch oven. Chicken, pork, or lamb may be substituted for beef, and other ingredients may be adjusted to taste. It works well either in a pit or above ground. If you like your veggies crispy, and you are cooking above ground, hold them out for the first 40 minutes of cooking; then add them. Otherwise, put them in for the entire cooking time.

Beef (1/2 pound per person)
1 large onion, sliced
1 potato per person (halved or sliced)
3 stalks celery
6 (or more) carrots
2 or 3 turnips
2 tomatoes (whole canned is okay)
1 head cabbage (optional)
2 to 3 garlic cloves (optional)
1 to 2 apples, sliced
Salt and pepper to taste
1/4 C. vegetable oil
1 C. hot water

Slice or dice the vegetables and set them aside. Rub salt and pepper into the meat. Garlic may be embedded in the roast or added separately.

Heat the oil in the oven (be sure it is level). Sear the meat on all sides, then wipe out excess oil. Slowly pour the water into the oven. Onions, with apple slices on top, may be attached to the roast with toothpicks or wood slivers. Add vegetables if you want them well cooked or are using a pit. Secure the lid on top of the oven and add coals on top of it.

If you are cooking above ground, replenish top and bottom coals as needed during cooking. If you are worried about veggies burning or sticking, twist the pot quickly a quarter turn every 15 minutes. Cook for one hour and check; if not done to your taste, cover and cook until it is.

Mulligan Stew

Because this recipe only works when cooked for a long period of time, it is best done in a pit.

All the vegetables you can find
Rabbit, chicken, or beef (in preferred order, about 1/2 pound
    of meat per person)
Salt and pepper to taste

Dice veggies and meat to about half–bite size. Put everything in the oven with enough water to cover 1/2 inch above ingredients. Put the oven in a very hot pit, cover it, and put coals on the lid. Bury with dirt for at least 8 hours.

The result is a delicious, homogeneous mass, packed with energy, that is too thick to eat with a spoon and too thin to eat with a fork. It is best slurped from a cup — just the thing to ingest at the end of a cold, wet, exhausting day. It goes especially well with Dutch oven biscuits.

Easy Biscuits

2 1/4 C. flour
1 tsp. salt
3 tsp. baking powder
About 3/4 C. milk (fresh or canned)
3/4 C. Crisco, lard, or cooking oil

Stir the dry ingredients together. Add milk, a little at a time, and stir until the ingredients are well blended and the dough is soft and malleable.

Heat the Dutch oven and melt the shortening. When it is hot (not smoking), drop in dollops of dough with a spoon or ladle. You can get golden tops by putting the lid on and adding a few coals, or you can leave the lid off and turn the biscuits. Depending on the heat, cooking time for flaky biscuits should be about 20 minutes. The recipe makes about 12 biscuits.

Bacon

Bacon is easy in a Dutch oven. If you have a side of bacon, slice it. If you have presliced bacon, there is no need to separate it. Drop it into a hot Dutch oven and stir it around with a long-handled fork until it is done to taste.

Fruit Cobbler

Peaches (fresh, canned, or frozen), sliced. For a 12-inch oven use two large
    cans (one will work); for a 14-inch oven, use 3 or 4 cans, or you can
    use pineapple, cherries, or berries
1 pkg. yellow cake mix
Water

Put the fruit into the Dutch oven, including juice if you are using canned or frozen fruit, and pour the dry cake mix on top.

If you are using fresh fruit, add just enough water to cover it. Stir 1/4 C. water into the cake mix and put it on top of the fruit.

Set the oven on coals, but do not add coals to the top. Bake for about 30 minutes, then check to see if it is done. Add coals sparingly to the lid for a browner top.

THE CUTTING EDGE: SHARPENING A KNIFE

THE CUTTING EDGE:
SHARPENING A KNIFE

Knife sharpening seems a pretty simple process. The blade is run at an angle (usually 20 to 25 degrees) across varying grades of sharpening stones until the blade edge becomes sharp enough to shave the hair on your arm.

But for most people, hair-cutting sharpness is elusive. At best, they achieve an edge that cuts a piece of paper and is soon dull again. That's because what they *really* achieve is a blade with a "wire edge" or "burr." Getting beyond the burr is necessary for true sharpness that will last. A little knowledge will help in that regard.

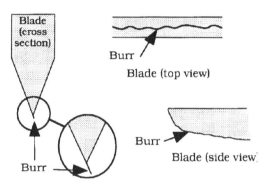

Successful knife sharpening is affected by a myriad of factors. The type of metal in the blade and the abrasive used to sharpen it are the two most influential.

TYPES OF KNIVES

Knives are made in many styles for various uses: filet knives, hunting knives, and pocketknives, to name a few. Specialty knives, such as kitchen knives with serrated edges, will not be discussed here.

The metal in knife blades, except Damascus, generally is either stainless steel (ATS-34 or 440V or C) or carbon steel. Stainless steel – the metal of choice among many knife makers today – is more difficult to sharpen than is carbon steel. But stainless steel is corrosion-resistant and, under some conditions, will hold an edge longer. Knife makers walk a fine line in searching for a steel that gives hardness for extended wear but is not too hard to sharpen or so brittle that the knife will break easily.

Some knives are subjected to differential heat treating to give the blade a hard edge with a tough spine that is not brittle. Sharpening this type of knife over time may remove all the edge-holding material to the extent that it can no longer be sharpened successfully.

TYPES OF SHARPENING STONES

There are many abrasive stones from which to choose. All will sharpen your knife to some degree, but choosing an improper one can make your job onerous and, in some cases, even ruin the blade.

There are two major types of stones: natural (materials found in nature) and manufactured (man-made abrasives or diamond). Natural stones, such as Arkansas and Washita, do a good job on carbon steel but do not perform well with stainless steel. If you are going to have only one set of stones, they probably should not be natural stones.

Manufactured stones are more versatile. Ceramic stones (made from aluminum oxide or silicon carbide) do well on everything except carbide tools. Diamond-impregnated stones will sharpen most things. As with anything else, the better the stones, the higher their price.

You can buy two-sided stones; generally they are coarse (180-grit) on one side and medium (320-grit) on the other. Two-sided stones will sharpen your blade but, because they lack a fine grit (600- to 800-grit), the edge will not last as long as one finished on a fine-grit stone.

There is a cheap way to avoid the expense of sharpening stones: silicone carbide sandpaper or SiC (often called "wet or dry"). The sandpaper, glued to a wooden block or piece of glass, will work as well as a stone. And you can have the equivalent of three stones – one in each grade of grit – for a small amount of cash outlay.

A rule of thumb:
Your stones should be at least as long as the
longest blade you will sharpen.

With time and improper use, stones can become degraded. Using a stone for a blade that is too short to span the stone's width will wear the stone unevenly until it has a hollowed center or an angled side and does not perform well.

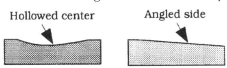

Hollowed center   Angled side

End Views of Single-Sided Stones

A stone can be damaged also if you sharpen only on part of the stone's length. Over time the surface becomes uneven and unfit for use.

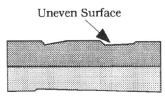

Uneven Surface

Side View of Two-Sided Stone

Stones are best used dry. Some people wet their stones with oil, saliva, or water. But be aware that the metal ground off the blade of your knife will fill the surface of a wetted stone until it will no longer grind at all – only hone. Honing is a final step in the sharpening process that is not effective without the preparatory grinding. Any lubricant on the stone distorts the "feel" of the grinding action. Maintaining a constant angle between the blade edge and the stone is difficult enough without introducing the variables that arise with lubrication.

ANGLES

Angles and geometric principles are as important to knife sharpening as they are to billiards. Once a new blade has been used enough that it becomes dull, it is quite easy to sharpen. With recurrent use and sharpening, however, the process becomes more difficult and less successful because it changes the angle of the edge on the blade.

New blades are beveled to a sharp edge (1). As they are used, the edge becomes rounded and dull (2). When a blade is sharpened, it is usually done on the very tip of the bevel. Each subsequent sharpening removes a small amount of steel and increases the edge angle (3, 4, 5). Eventually getting a sharp edge becomes impossible. The edge angle has become so wide that the blade itself must be reshaped to recreate the basic edge (6).

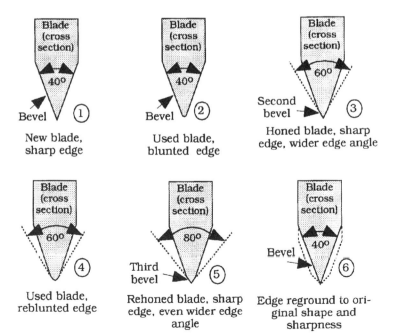

New blade, sharp edge

Used blade, blunted edge

Honed blade, sharp edge, wider edge angle

Used blade, reblunted edge

Rehoned blade, sharp edge, even wider edge angle

Edge reground to original shape and sharpness

Two angles are of vital importance in sharpening knives effectively. The first angle to be concerned about is the angle between the knife handle and the outside edge of the stone. Keep it at about 45 degrees.

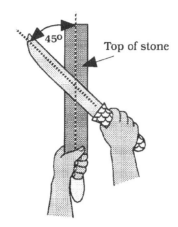

The second angle is the relationship between the blade and the flat surface of the stone – the angle should be 20 degrees, more or less, depending on the blade configuration.

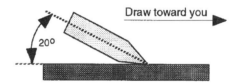

To help you set and keep exact angles, angle guides may be purchased. Each has its own strengths and weaknesses and they are not inexpensive. Perhaps the best for use with a bench stone is the Buck HoneMaster; unfortunately it is no longer made. Sometimes with luck and determination, one can be found for sale secondhand in a knife shop or thrift store. You may also purchase a system of stones, such as Lansky or GATCO that come with guides and directions. With a little practice and patience, you can do the job without these expensive (and, sometimes, not too accurate) systems.

SHARPENING

When you sharpen, you are setting out to grind the blade to its original (40-degree) edge and then create a new bevel to make it sharp.

The basic method of working the blade is to keep its edge in contact with the stone and draw the knife toward you. Although you can sharpen a blade anywhere, it is easiest if you lay the stone on a flat surface such as a workbench. As it travels along the stone, the blade should slide to grind its entire length. Keep a firm, steady pressure, but don't be abusive. If you maintain the 45-degree angle, the action will grind the blade evenly from hilt to point. To work the other side, keep the respective angles, turn the knife over, and push the blade away from you.

Your first objective is to remove the old edge. If the blade has been abused and has large nicks in it, you will start with a coarse stone (180-grit). This will leave some pretty deep scratches, so it's best to use the coarse stone just enough to get the nicks out.

You may have been taught that the way to sharpen a blade is to try to "shave a thin layer" off the stone. This is not a good idea because you will not hold a constant angle when you do that. Different edges require different angles. What happens when you try to "shave" is that, operating by feel and hearing, you instinctively raise and lower the edge to make things "feel" right.

The best way is to take a light stroke and check to see that you are holding the blade at the correct angles. If the scratches show only on the front edge of the bevel, you have too much angle (greater than 20 degrees); if they show only on the back edge, you have too little angle (less than 20 degrees). When scratches are centered on the bevel, you have it just right. If you have trouble seeing the scratches, try blackening the blade with Magic Marker or tool dye.

Work one side of the blade until you have removed the old edge. Continue working the edge until you have raised a small burr. The burr will appear on the side of the blade *opposite* the side you are working. Keep the burr as small as you can. Practice will help. Turn the blade over and grind an equal amount off the other side.

Now go to the medium (320- to 360-grit) stone. At this stage, you are not so much grinding away metal as you are removing the scratch marks made by the coarse stone. Work one side until the coarse scratch pattern is gone, then do an equal amount of work on the other side. You will still have a wire edge and, if you look closely (a magnifying glass may be necessary), you will see very fine scratch marks. The blade may seem sharp – it will cut paper – and this is where most people quit. That is the reason their sharp edge doesn't cut hair or last very long.

You can roll the blade edge up a little and try a couple "slicing-off-the-stone" strokes. This will give you a bevel edge with microscopic 320- to 360-grit serrations – good enough for most work. But if you want to shave with the blade or have an edge that will last a long time, you are not done.

Go to your fine (600- to 800-grit) stone and hone – that is, wipe the blade opposite from the grinding stroke, alternating sides with each stroke. You will have to go onto the edge and stroke lightly. It only takes a few licks per side. The object is to remove any burr you may have left, but not to round the edge.

Try shaving the hair on your arm. If the blade doesn't cut the hair, check the edge for roughness with the ball of your thumb. If roughness is present, go back to the medium stone. If there is no roughness, but the edge doesn't cut hair, continue with the fine-grit stone until it does.

For a longer-lasting edge than that provided by the method above, you will want to use the multi- or final-bevel technique. This is done with the fine-grit stone. Proceed as you did when you started with the coarse-grit stone but raise the angle of the blade to a 25- or even 30-degree angle.

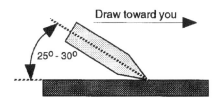

Draw toward you

$25^0 - 30^0$

Alternating sides, give each side about five licks, starting with firm pressure on the first stroke and lessening the pressure until the fifth stroke is very light. Should you raise a burr, which is unlikely, work it out by honing as you did before. Test the knife for sharpness and work it until you are satisfied. The final bevel edge will last longer and be a little sharper than the standard edge, but the knife will require more work to sharpen when the edge finally becomes dull.

MAKING A
GOURD
CANTEEN

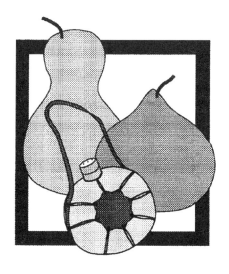

MAKING A GOURD CANTEEN

A gourd canteen is historically accurate for many periods of reenactment, and it is practical, surprisingly durable, and easy to make.

There are two ways to acquire a suitable gourd: buying one or growing one. Buying one is by far the easiest. Prices for a good canteen gourd can run between $7 and $15 (during the 1998 rendezvous season, they were selling for about $1 per diameter-inch).

Gourds may be purchased from many places (see suppliers, for just a few). Be sure the gourd you buy is the size you want. It should be already dried – light tan to white in color and very light in weight. Some discoloration is natural because, during the drying process, gourds often develop an exterior mold. If you don't like the discoloration, you often can remove it with steel wool or fine sandpaper.

You may want to grow gourds, keep what you want, and sell the rest. The seeds usually can be obtained from the listed suppliers. Your garden should be fertilized, well-drained, and in a sunny location. Gourds will require a lot of water during hot weather.

Gourds have a long growing season. Plants need at least 140 days to mature. Presoaking the seeds and scarring them with a knife blade will encourage them to sprout sooner. Gourds don't transplant well, so start the seeds in peat pots. Seedlings should be set in rows 5 feet apart, plants within rows need to be 2 feet apart. If you use the hill method of planting, the hills should be 5 feet apart with 2 plants per hill. Gourds are vines like melons and cucumbers and will spread out as they grow. Prune the vines, especially the lead runners, when they are 8 to 10 feet long to encourage branching and female flowers. It is helpful to put all but heavy gourds on trellises; it prevents pests, rotting, and distortion.

Frost can kill them. Gourds should be harvested when the stems turn brown; leave a couple of inches of stem attached. Store them in a well-ventilated, dark or shaded area such as a garage or shed. Don't allow them to touch each other.

Drying to a hard shell takes a long time – up to nine months for large gourds. Keep your gourds in a warm, dark place with good ventilation. Turn them weekly. To prevent the formation of mold during drying, wipe them with a solution of 2 tablespoons of bleach per gallon of water. When they are dry, they are very lightweight and you should be able to hear the seeds rattle when you shake the gourd.

Drying may be hastened by cutting a hole in them; this also reduces the risk of rotting. Because you are going to turn your favorite into a canteen anyway, you may want to cut a hole in that one. And green gourds have less chance of splitting when drilled or cut than do dry ones.

MATERIALS

To make your canteen, you will need:

    Gourd (6-inch diameter is ideal)
    1-inch and 3/8-inch dowels for wood stopper
    Steel wool or sandpaper
    Shellac, varnish, or wax for outside
    12 ounces of beeswax (or epoxy resin) to coat inside
    Stick and pebbles or sand to clean out seeds
    Harness or pouch materials

CLEANING AND PREPARING THE GOURD

Wash the outside of the gourd in warm, soapy water and use steel wool or sandpaper to remove the mold and the thin outside skin. You may need to file down the stem until it is flush with the gourd. Be careful not to "ding" the gourd itself.

Choose the location where you want your stopper. Cut a 1 inch hole centered on the rounded side of the gourd. *Be very careful how much pressure you apply to cut the hole or drill it,* especially if the gourd is dry. Dry gourds are extremely susceptible to splitting and chipping. If it does split or chip, it may be repairable with an epoxy resin.

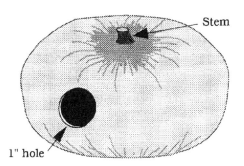

Stem

1" hole

Loosen the seeds and other inside debris with a stick or the handle of a wooden spoon inserted into the hole. Shake out the seeds, dry them, and store them for future use. Make sure all the fibrous tissue is removed from the inside. If the stick is not enough to achieve this, pour in some coarse sand or small pebbles, shake the contents until you are sure the inside is smooth, and dump them out. If you don't clear out all the "gunk" inside, sooner or later — no matter what you coat the inside with — the water from the canteen will taste bad.

Dry the gourd completely over several days and apply a coat of shellac, varnish, or wax to the outside.

FINISHING THE CANTEEN

The 1-inch hole can be plugged with a cork, a corncob, or other material. It is more functional, however, if you make a wooden insert that has its own plug. The insert is sealed when the beeswax or epoxy resin is applied to the inside of the canteen. A gourd canteen with a wooden plug and stopper is a more secure vessel than one with a single-plug system. With a single plug, the seal is necessarily broken each time the stopper is removed and the pressures of removing and replacing the plug can chip the edge of the hole.

A plug system can be as personalized as hand-whittled ivory, but a simple plug can be made from hardwood dowels (dowel sizes may vary depending on your gourd and preference, but 1-inch and 3/8-inch dowels work well for canteens).

Cut two 1-inch lengths from a 1-inch dowel. Drill a 3/8-inch hole completely through the center of one piece and a 3/8-inch hole halfway through the center of the other. Cut a 1 1/2-inch length from a 3/8-inch dowel.

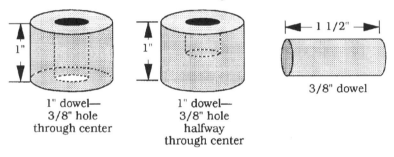

1" dowel—
3/8" hole
through center

1" dowel—
3/8" hole
halfway
through center

3/8" dowel

Glue the piece of 3/8-inch dowel into the 1-inch dowel with the halfway hole. You may want to round off the protruding end of the smaller dowel and lightly sand the plug parts, but don't sand the 3/8-inch dowel much; you want a snug fit.

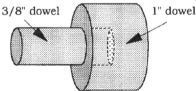

3/8" dowel

1" dowel

Glue the other piece of 1-inch dowel into the 1-inch hole in the gourd. You now have a serviceable plug that will put little strain on the gourd.

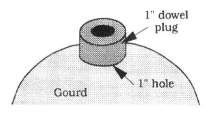

1" dowel
plug

1" hole

Gourd

To prevent loss, the upper part of the plug may be attached to the lower with a length of sinew, small cord, or small chain. You may even decorate it with beads.

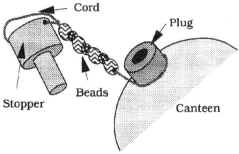

Epoxy resin or a similar chemical can be used to coat the inside of the canteen. If you are a reenactor, there is only one proper coating – beeswax. Beeswax is readily available from leather and craft supply stores.

In a pan, heat enough wax to coat the inside of the canteen walls until it is liquified – overkill is better than skimping. A 12-ounce amount is best (four 3-ounce blocks). Beeswax doesn't cost all that much and the overage is recoverable. Don't overheat it because even beeswax has a flashpoint. Warm the gourd. Pour in the melted beeswax. Roll the gourd around to ensure full coverage, then empty out the excess. Let the gourd cool.

MAKING A HARNESS

There are many styles of harnesses for gourd canteens. Some are merely leather pouches with the canteen inserted inside. Others become integral to the canteen itself. You can copy one of the styles below, use your imagination to modify them, or come up with an idea that works better for you.

The first harness has two leather patches, with holes in each point. One patch is centered on each side of the canteen. The patches are attached with artificial sinew loops (or waxed, nylon string) to a 3/4-inch-wide shoulder strap. The shoulder strap goes around the circumference of the canteen and has seven equidistant holes punched midway across the strap width to receive the sinew loops from the patches. The eighth (uppermost) point of each patch is attached with sinew wrapped around the plug. This harness becomes an integral part of the canteen.

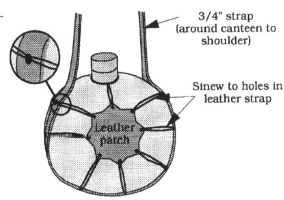

An alternate harness is essentially just a sling. One strap goes around the diameter of the canteen. A shoulder strap is riveted to the diameter strap and wraps around the bottom circumference of the canteen. A third strap is riveted to the shoulder strap at the bottom of the canteen and is at right angles to it and riveted to the diameter strap. This harness is not permanent; the canteen may be removed easily, sometimes too easily.

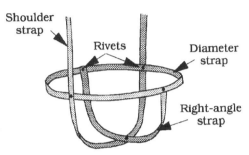

A third possibility is to put your canteen in a leather pouch. Although it will stay in place, it is not as accessible as it is in a harness.

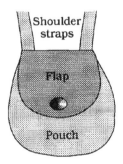

A FINAL NOTE

Your canteen should always be kept at least partially full of water. If left empty for any appreciable time, the beeswax will dry out and flake off. If your water suddenly starts tasting moldy, some beeswax is missing. In that case, dry out the canteen thoroughly, use a stick to knock out the loose wax, and reapply more wax.

Your canteen, if treated properly, will provide you with cool, good-tasting water for a long, long time.

Salud!

ADDENDUM: MAKING AN OLLA (WATER JUG)

The same principles for making a canteen can apply to make a very serviceable water jug for camp use. The gourd should be large enough to hold at least a gallon of water. Several types of gourds besides large canteen gourds make good ollas:

Bilobal

Teardrop Bule

The hole is cut around where the stem is attached and may be larger than 1 inch. The steps to making a canteen apply to an olla. The harness can be adapted from the sling harness or woven with artificial sinew or leather thong. You can use your imagination to come up with patterns that please you.

BUILDING
YOUR OWN
BUCKSAW

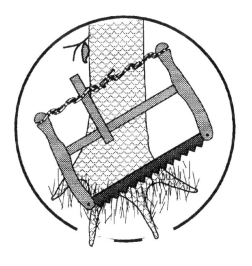

BUILDING YOUR OWN BUCKSAW

It is hard to imagine a piece of outdoor equipment that is handier than a saw; a good one has a variety of uses. The problem is to find one that can be taken down easilty and transported, yet is large enough to do heavy jobs. There are some small ones around – fragile things that won't cut wood any larger than branches easily broken by hand. They often are equipped with a 14-inch blade and won't cut serious downfall or significant firewood.

The ideal camp saw is rugged, has a 21- to 22-inch blade, and is readily disassembled and packed. This pattern makes a saw that will do a variety of tasks without wearing out itself or user. It can be constructed by using only hand tools, but a power router and jigsaw surely come in handy.

MATERIALS

Hardwood board(s) large enough to allow finished dimensions (FDs) given below (see also **Figure 1**):
Two braces, each 14 1/2 inches x 2 1/4 inches x 3/4 inch
One crossbuck, 19 inches x 1 1/8 inches x 3/4 inch
One shiv, 8 inches x 1 inch x 1/4 inch

Piece of rope about 4 1/2 feet long
21-inch saw blade
Two nails or rivets
Wood stain (optional)
Finishing material, e.g., linseed oil, Deft, polyurethane

Use hardwood for all the component parts. Often cabinet shops have give-away waste pieces large enough to build the saw. Cut-off nails will suffice for pins, but round-headed rivets look nicer. The rope should be smooth, like clothesline stock or other tightly woven cotton. Hemp-style rope will soon break from the unrelenting tension and twist. Most hardware stores carry good blades, such as the "Made in Denmark" Distan brand, that cost well under five dollars.

MAKING THE PATTERN

It is useful to draw out a pattern on paper first. That way you will have two identical braces, and you have the pattern to make other saws should you want to do so. Draw the pattern according to **Figure 1** (you need to draw only one brace as the two are identical). Place the pieces on the hardwood board (lengthwise of grain) and trace around them. Cut out the saw pieces along your lines.

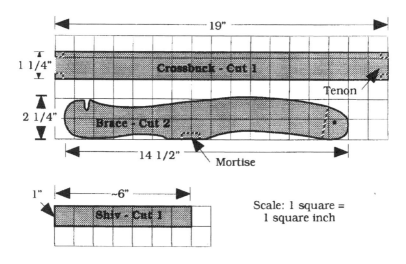

Figure 1. Patterns for Wood Saw Pieces

MAKING THE SAW

Cut a mortise in the side of each brace. The placement of the mortise is important. It should be 3/8 inch deep, 7/8 inch long, and 7/16 inch wide. Center it between the edges and the breakovers. Make certain to place both mortises identically in the two braces.

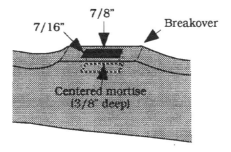

If you use power tools, each mortise can be inlet with a router or drill bit and the ends squared off with a file or chisel. Alternatively, you can leave the hole with rounded corners and sand off the crossbuck tenons to fit.

In each brace (the end opposite the notched end), drill a hole the diameter of your rivets or nail shanks. Place the hole 5/8 inch up from the notched edge and 3/4 inch in from the end.

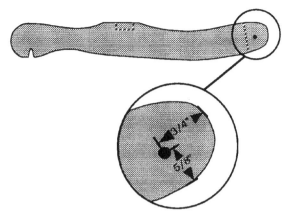

Cut a thin slit in the end with the hole. Place the slit halfway between the edges and carry it past the hole for the pin. The blade will slide down into the slit and be held in place with the pin through the hole.

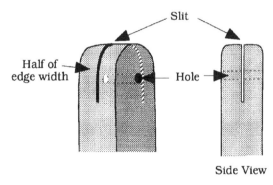

Side View

Cut the tenon on both ends of the crossbuck. Center the tenon on the end, making each 7/8 inch by 7/16 inch. When you have sanded them, they should fit into the brace mortises snugly, but not tightly. If you have round mortise corners, round off the tenons to match.

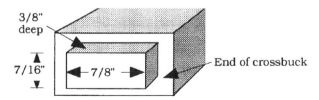

Once the saw is cut and detailed, sand it to a smooth finish. You may want to round corners and edges to make it comfortable to handle. Apply a stain (if you choose to use one) and a protective finish to the wood. If you apply linseed oil and intend to use the saw for more than a few minutes at a time, you'll need gloves when you saw. Linseed oil can cause the wood to really "grip" bare hands and raise some fearsome blisters.

ASSEMBLING THE SAW FOR USE

Place the tenons of the crossbar into the mortises of the braces, notched edges to the outside (1). Place the blade into the slits in the braces, align the blade with the holes and put the nails or rivets through the holes to hold the blade in place (2). Trim any excess off the rivets until they protrude only slightly on the opposite side.

Put the rope through the notches and tie the two ends together (3). Insert the shiv between the ropes and use it to twist the rope quite snugly (4); this will put tension on the blade to keep it in place. To hold the twist, push the end of the shiv toward the crossbuck until it overlaps (5).

Notches
(1) Tenons inserted in mortises
Rivets or nails
(2) Blade inserted in slit; rivets through holes
(3) Rope tied around notches
(4) Shiv between ropes. Twist by turning end over end
(5) Twisted rope held by shiv on crossbuck

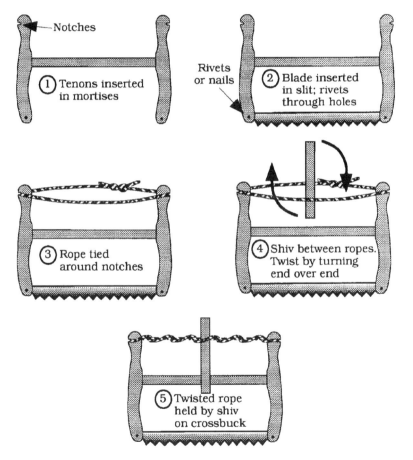

You will find this saw to be light, sturdy, and large enough to do a significant amount of work. It can be carried in a backpack or on a horse. It takes up little room and will prove itself many times over.

ADDENDUM: MAKING A BAG FOR YOUR SAW

Use a good canvas of at least 10-ounce weight. Cut a piece 27 inches x 7 1/2 inches. Fold the canvas in half lengthwise and sew a double seam 1/2 inch in from the side and across one end (bottom). Sew a 1/2-inch hem at the top. Turn the bag inside out.

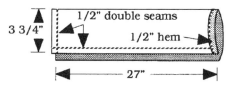

Cut a piece of 1-inch-wide twill tape (or other heavy tape) 30 inches long. Mark the center. Sew the center midway across one side of the bag 1 inch down from the hemmed top.

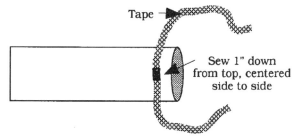

When the saw is packed inside, fold the top of the bag over the contents so the tape is on the outside. Wrap the tape around the bag and tie it.

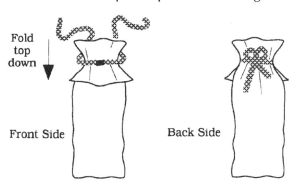

You may want to make a small bag to fit inside to hold the rivets or nails to keep them from getting lost. You also may want to lay in a piece of leather, a bag, or another piece of canvas to wrap around the saw blade; the extra protection will cut down on damage from the teeth.

MAKING
LAZYBACKS

MAKING LAZYBACKS

Reginald and Gladys Laubin, in their classic book, *The Indian Tipi*, call the lazy-back "the most important article of furniture in a tipi." Indeed the willow chair offers a number of advantages. Besides augmenting ambiance with color and decoration, it is extremely comfortable and very supportive. Moreover, it takes up little space and can be used as an elevated bed or rolled into a tight, light bundle for easy storage and transport.

There are two basic parts to the lazyback — poles several feet in length that form the tripod support and a tapered mat made of peeled willow withes tied or strung together in snug rows. To achieve that end, there are several systems. Three are presented here.

Method 1 drills holes through the willows so four sinew strings thread through each willow straight up the lazyback; this method takes less sinew and, except for drilling the holes, is quick to do. If you want to do it as the Native Americans did it, use an awl. Because you are drilling holes, you must use relatively thick willows. The chair is quite fragile and repairing a broken willow is somewhat difficult.

Method 2 wraps the sinew around the willows. This method is also completed quickly and repairs are easy (all you have to do is slide in a new willow), but the chairs will not tolerate much heavy use.

Method 3 ties in each willow as you build up the chair. This method is the most time-consuming and makes the chair difficult to repair, but it gives the most long-lasting and sturdy result.

Which method you use depends on your personal choice. You need to consider the time in construction, durability, available materials, and ease of repair.

We recommend you use a frame. But in the wild, you can make do by using stakes driven into reasonably level ground. The measurements given are average — you can adjust them to suit the effect you want. Cheyenne and Sioux lazybacks were quite short and wide; those of the Crow and Blackfoot were tall and quite narrow.

MATERIALS

To make an average-size lazyback you will need:

For assembling it on the ground:
Eight small, but sturdy, stakes

For assembling it with a frame:
A piece of 1/2-inch or 3/4-inch plywood about 6 feet long and 32 inches wide
Two furring strips, cut to about 1 inch x 1/2 inch. One should be 19 inches long, the other, just over 6 feet long

Eight good-sized nails (you can use finish nails or cut the heads off box nails once they are in place)

Screws or nails to attach boards to plywood (a little glue helps)

For the lazyback:

275-300 straight willows, about 3 1/2 feet long and about the diameter of a pencil in the middle of the length (larger for Method 1)

Artificial sinew - about 9 yards for Method 1, 16 yards for Method 2, or 45 yards for Method 3

6 inch-wide strip(s) of trade wool, buckskin, or flannel. Bound edges depend on the style of chair you make (pp. 79, 82). For binding four edges, one strip 17 feet long is best, but you can use pieces. To bind only the sides, you need two strips, each about 6 1/4 feet long

Paint for decoration (if desired)

1 foot of 8- to 10-ounce leather for tripod strap

Knife or other implement for stripping bark

Awl or drill with small bit (Method 1)

For the tripod:

Three straight poles 4 to 5 feet long, with about a 2-inch diameter at the butt end. One should be slightly longer than the others and will form the center pole

Leather thong to tie poles together

Knife, if you want carved poles

LAZYBACK STYLES

In the directions that follow, the lazybacks are described with measurements that approximate those of the Crow or Blackfoot. Their lazybacks are relatively long and skinny. You may choose to make one more typical of the Sioux and Cheyenne, which are wider and shorter. If so, adjust your measurements accordingly.

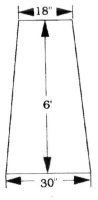

Crow or Blackfoot

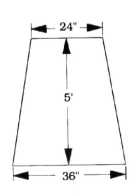

Sioux or Cheyenne

MAKING A GROUND FRAME

Drive four stakes into the ground in a straight line and 5 inches apart (total distance is 15 inches). This forms the top of the ground layout. Now draw a 30-inch line on the ground 6 feet from the stakes and parallel to them. Center the line on the line of stakes, allowing the ends to extend 6 inches beyond each end of the stakes. Divide the line into thirds (9-inch segments) and drive stakes into the ends of the line and into the 9-inch markers. This forms the bottom of the ground layout.

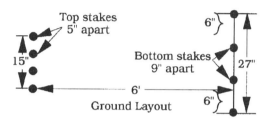

MAKING A PLYWOOD FRAME

Draw two parallel lines on the plywood 6 feet apart. At the approximate center of the board, draw a line intersecting the two parallel lines and perpendicular to them. At the top, make two marks, one 9 1/2 inches to the right of the intersecting line, the other 9 1/2 inches to the left of the line. At the bottom, make two similar marks to the right and left of the line, 15 1/2 inches from the intersecting line. Connect the left marks and right marks from top to bottom with a heavy line. Cut the board along the outside lines.

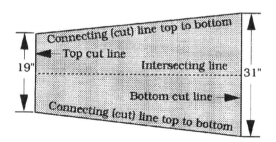

Cut plywood frame

Measuring from the left end (or right end if you're left-handed), mark the 19-inch furring strip at 2 1/2 inches, 7 1/2 inches, 12 1/2 inches, and 17 1/2 inches. Cut 1/4-inch-deep slots at those points across the 1-inch width. Attach the furring to the top of the plywood, edges flush, slots up.

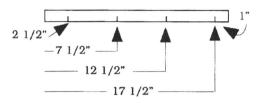

Abut the 6-foot furring (1-inch side up) against the 19-inch furring, placing it one the left side of the plywood (right side if you're left-handed); the inside corner of the abutment should be 1 1/2 inches from the first slot on the left (or right, for lefties). Screw or nail the 6-foot furring in place.

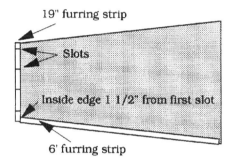

Put four nails partway into the top of the frame, even with the slots. Near the bottom of the frame, put four more nails in the face of the plywood (spaced from the furred edge) at 2 1/2 inches, 11 1/2 inches, 20 1/2 inches, and 29 1/2 inches. Cut off the nail heads so you can remove the strings easily when the chair is completed.

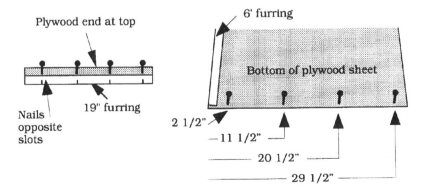

Cut the sinew into four equal lengths. Tie one end of each to a bottom stake (ground layout) or nail (frame). Skip to Selecting Willows if you're going to use Method 1.

For Method 2, tie each sinew to the bottom nail or stake. Take the loose end to the top, wrap it around the corresponding top stake or nail, return to the bottom, and tie it firmly to the beginning stake or nail. Don't cut the sinew. These are your support thongs. Keep the doubled strands very snug. Wind the loose ends into secure balls that you can unwind as you weave them between the willows.

For Method 3, tie each sinew to the bottom nail or stake. Take each loose end to its top stake or nail, return to the bottom and tie it, but don't cut the sinew. Keep these two wraps very snug when you tie them off. Wind the remaining sinew (about 22 feet per strand) into four balls to unwind as you weave them between the willows.

SELECTING AND PREPARING THE WILLOWS

Select straight, even willows with a diameter the size of a pencil near the middle of the length (larger if you are using Method 1). The willows can arc in an easy curve, but avoid those with kinks. Cut them to allow a length of 3 1/2 feet or longer. Cut more than you need, as some will not be usable.

It is best to cut them when the sap is running (spring and fall) because they peel more easily. Peel them when you cut them – if you wait until later, they are very difficult to peel and the final product will be rougher. Green withes can be soaked in water if you want to put off peeling for a while. You may want to leave a few unpeeled to use in creating a pattern (add them in as you go up the chair).

Straighten the peeled willows as much as you can with your hands, then bind them in small tight bundles to keep them from warping. Place the bundles in a cool shady place so the willows do not dry too fast.

Once they are completely dry, take the bundles apart. Trim the knobs from the branch joints and make the willows as smooth as possible. Any that are not straight enough can be soaked and straightened again. Tying them into position, however, will straighten all but the really crooked ones.

For any method, place the willows with a thick end next to a small end, alternating as you move up the chair.

Guidelines for the ground layout are the two outside strings. Willows should extend 1 1/2 inches beyond them on both sides when the lazyback is finished. You may want to allow a little more as you put them in so later you can trim them even.

The guidelines for the wood frame are the 6-foot furring strip on the outside of the frame (willows are abutted to it) and the plywood edge on the opposite side. On the open side, extend the willows to the edge or a little beyond so you can trim them later.

For any method, you will work from the bottom to the top.

INCORPORATING DECORATION

You may decorate the lazyback as you weave the willows. Many tribes wove two colored (trade) cloth strips between the willows starting about halfway up the total length of the chair and dividing the chair into thirds or fourths from side to side. The strips should be about 2 inches wide and about 18 inches longer than from where you start to the top of the chair (you can trim any excess later).

Cut a notch in the bottom end of each strip and leave 5 or 6 inches hanging down on the front side of the willows. Add about four more willows in front of the strip, then four willows behind the strip, then four in front, and so forth to the top. In-and-out more often than every four willows will cause them to bow. A good trick is to hold up the strips with a rubber band attached to the top of the frame. The band holds the strips in place and makes it easy to keep them straight.

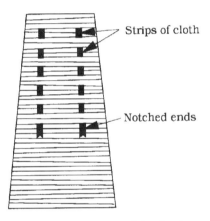

Strips of cloth

Notched ends

Strips of cloth woven into finished lazyback

The Sioux and Cheyenne put four (usual) or six sections of red and/or green painted willows near the top of their chairs and added tassels.

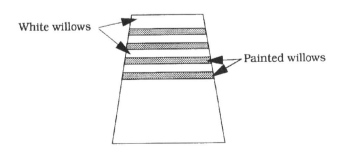

White willows

Painted willows

TYING THE WILLOWS IN PLACE

Method 1

Lay the first willow at the bottom end against the stakes or nails, allowing for end extensions. With a very sharp, thin tool like an awl or a very small drill bit, make holes in the willow where it crosses the strings. Be sure the willow doesn't rotate as you make the holes. Thread the willow on the four strings.

Continue in the same way with the remaining willows, alternating narrow and wide ends, as you build your way up the lazyback. Allow some play between the willows. If they are too snug, the lazyback will wear out quickly and the strings will break.

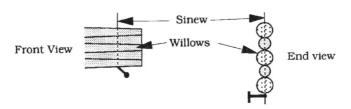

When you are about 5 inches from the top of the layout or frame, tie off the top willow with a sturdy knot.

Method 2

Place the first willow at the bottom end under the double vertical sinew against the stakes or nails, allowing for 1 1/2-inch end extensions. Bring the loose end of the sinew behind the willow, up over the front of the vertical strand, and back to the rear. Repeat for all four strands, using each loose end in turn.

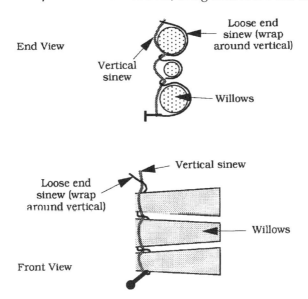

Place the second willow, alternating wide and narrow ends, against the first and wrap it in the same way. Repeat for remaining willows, fitting them snugly against the preceding one and the sinew tight. When you are about 5 inches from the top of the layout or frame, tie off the loose-end sinews and vertical strands with secure knots.

Method 3

Place the first willow at the bottom end *on top of both vertical strands.* Snug it up against the stakes or nails and allow for 1 1/2-inch end extensions. Bring the loose end of the sinew over the willow, back around both vertical strands (Step 1), around to the front, and under the wrapped strand (Step 2). Repeat for the other three strands using each loose end in turn. For the first five or six willows at the bottom and the last five or six at the top, you may want to tie two knots in each location to anchor them very securely. You also may opt to use a half-hitch, though the knots are bulkier.

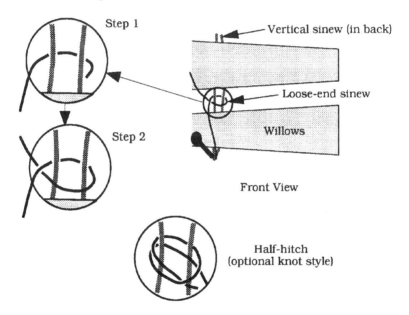

Step 1

Vertical sinew (in back)

Loose-end sinew

Step 2

Willows

Front View

Half-hitch
(optional knot style)

When you are about 5 inches from the top, tie off the loose ends and the vertical strands with a secure knot.

COMPLETING THE WILLOWS

Remove the willows from the frame. Draw a line across the willows from top to bottom 1 1/2 inches out from the outside vertical sinew. With a sharp saw, clippers, or whatever works best for you, trim away any excess so the ends of the willows are a consistent 1 1/2 inches from the sinew from top to bottom. If you use a saw, you may want to clamp two boards on either side of the willows to hold them securely while you saw. You may also trim the withes on a table saw that has a fine-toothed blade.

Binding the edges of your lazyback with strips of trade cloth, buckskin, or flannel adds stability and longevity. The Crow bound their chairs all the way around; the Blackfoot bound only the sides. The Cheyenne and Sioux used no binding.

Turn under the raw edges of the binding about 1/2 inch. Fold the binding in half and wrap it around the edges of the lazyback and over the vertical sinew that's tying the willows in place. Sew the binding in place with sinew, going between the willows, to the inside of the vertical sinew, and through all binding thicknesses. If you are going all the way around with a continuous strip, make snug 90-degree corners; it is also best to begin the binding at the top center of the chair.

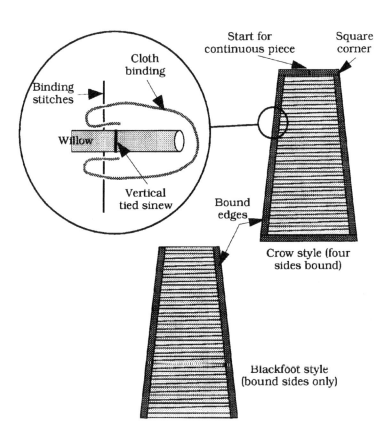

Cut a strap out of the leather. Sew it on the top center of the lazyback, leaving a loop to wrap over the tripod. Stitches should wrap around the willows on the back side.

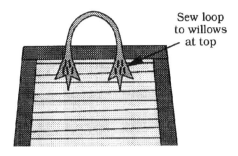

Sew loop
to willows
at top

MAKING THE TRIPOD

You can decorate the tripod poles by leaving some bark in attractive patterns along their length. If you do not want bark decoration, you should strip all the bark off. You can paint or decorate the bare portions to the limits of your creativity and preferences.

There are several methods of securing a tripod. One is the same as that for a tipi; it is very stable. Tie the three tripod poles together as shown below.

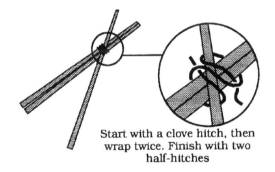

Start with a clove hitch, then
wrap twice. Finish with two
half-hitches

The second method is less secure. You may want to set the poles in the ground to stabilize them. Wrap the poles with thong:

A third method, the one most commonly found in museums, makes a tripod that is very easy to control. Drill holes through all three poles at an equal distance from the bottom. Tie all three together with a leather thong, center pole in the middle.

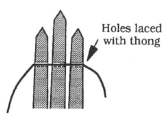

Holes laced with thong

Spread your tripod with the two short poles toward the front and the support pole to the back. Hang the leather loop of the backrest over the back pole of the tripod so the sides are supported by the poles and you have two feet or so to sit on.

For added stability, thread a thong through the willows near the base of the back of the lazyback. Go up three or four willows and thread it through again. Tie the thong to the support poles.

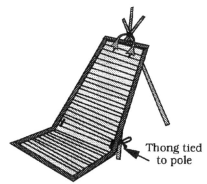

Thong tied to pole

Admire your fine effort and enjoy your comfortable chair!

MAKING
MOUNTAIN
MAN
SNOWSHOES

MAKING MOUNTAIN MAN SNOWSHOES

The early Indians made and used snowshoes designed to fit the conditions in whichever part of the country they called home, often creating several different styles. For instance, one of the shoes used by the Penobscots of Maine, who had to walk in brushy terrain, had a square snub nose. Made of ash, it was flat and quite wide and had a short tail section.

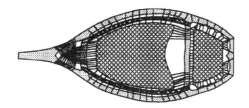

The northern bands of Chippewa used a number of styles suited to the varied land over which they roamed, ranging from a "bear paw" to the familiar "pickerel" shape.

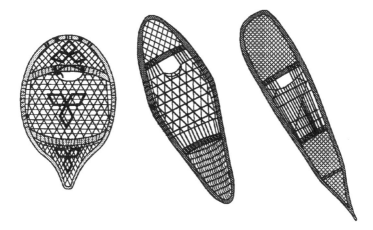

Indians used wood that was dictated by what grew in their geographical area: usually spruce, birch, or ash. Webbing was often *babiche* — partly tanned skin cut into thin strips. The mountain man snowshoe illustrated here is based on museum pieces and on paintings, drawings, and descriptions in journals left by early white explorers among the Indians. As was common with many Indian snowshoes, the toe is bent upward to help keep it from catching in loose snow or brush and tripping the wearer; the rear is a tail that keeps the shoe from "kicking" upward (throwing weighty snow on the webbing and the user's legs) and provides stability.

Indian styles of webbing varied from intricate to crude and utilitarian. The webbing used here is patterned after a simple Indian working shoe designed for use on crust or in powder, in clear or brushy areas.

Whether you are upgrading historical equipment, just having fun creating something of your own, or are in a survival situation, these snowshoes work well and look good. If properly cared for, they will provide many years of hard use and enjoyment. They are a style that has come to be known as Ojibwan or Chippewan. Although the directions are not for an emergency circumstance, the knowledge you gain should enable you to make a pair of snowshoes that will work well enough to meet survival conditions.

For instance, should you be stranded in a vehicle, the floor mats can be cut into strips and used in place of rawhide. Whatever wood is handy will make a temporary frame and it need not be an elongated one — a circular or "bear paw" style might fit the bill. In another situation, small green branches or withes can be woven into a mesh and secured through holes burned in the frame with the heated tang of a belt buckle. A belt cut into several lengthwise pieces could serve for toe and heel straps. All this, of course, supposes that you don't go naked into danger and that you always carry a serviceable pocketknife and a flint-and-steel fire starting kit or other means of making a fire.

MATERIALS

To make a pair of snowshoes, you will need:

For snowshoes:
Plank (2+ inches thick x dimensions of your shoes)
Two pieces of hardwood [1 inch x 11 1/2 inches x 2 inches (or less)]
Saplings or wood strips for frame (pp. 91-92)
Small pieces of scrap lumber
Several long screws
20 to 22 feet of 1/8-inch lacing or rawhide
30 to 32 feet of 1/4-inch lacing or rawhide
Clamps
Sandpaper
Spar varnish

For bindings (Figures 6 and 7):
Heavy leather 8 inches x 12 inches
8 feet of rawhide or leather thong lacing
Leather straps, 5/8 inch x up to 6 feet, depending on type of binding
Buckles
Leather rivets (or use rawhide)
Leather punch

TIPS THAT MAY HELP
The following suggestions may make your work easier:

1. If your frame wood is less than perfect (e.g., minor knots), it can be bound in wet rawhide before you begin bending it. This should stop the wood from breaking when stressed.

2. Bend one side of the frame at a time to put it under the spreaders. Resist the temptation to bend both sides together.

3. Once the frame pieces are under the spreaders, they can be held firmly in place by inserting a screw next to each piece where it begins to bend outward.

4. Bark may be left on the frame pieces for a quicker pair of shoes, such as in an emergency. If you can, however, the bottom edges should be smoothed off.

5. To eliminate confusion during webbing, it may help to trace the frame on paper and lay out the webbing steps before you start lacing.

6. The shaded strand in the middle section of webbing may be dyed with aniline dye or other coloring substance. It will give the shoes an added bit of decoration and it helps you see what you are doing.

PREPARING MATERIALS

The tools to make the snowshoes can be as elaborate as those a full-scale wood shop would have or as simple as a pole axe, hand saw, and pocketknife. The directions assume that you have some common tools available. If not, you will have to use ingenuity born of desperation, keeping in mind that the early Indians made shoes with nothing more than stone or soft copper knives and drills. Although we no longer live under those limitations, we will make use of relatively simple technologies.

Webbing. Although "boot lace" leather can be used for webbing, standard rawhide is better. Many stores or traders who deal in leather will supply rawhide strips at a reasonable price. Two excellent ones are listed in the supplier section.

If you have to cut the leather into strips yourself, a lace-cutting tool can be bought at most leather craft supply stores or you can make a simple one. Get a piece of wood 1 x 1 x 5 inches. Cut a square notch out of the center twice as deep as the strips you want. Insert a razor or box knife blade in the wood one-half the height of the notch (distance from blade to bottom of notch is the width you want). Bind the ends of the blade in place with rawhide or sinew.

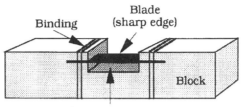

Binding

Blade
(sharp edge)

Block

Width of strip between blade and
bottom of notch (e.g., 1/4")

Pick a piece of rawhide (softened with water) or leather about 8 inches in diameter; cut a starter piece in the center the width of your cutter. Insert it between the blade and the bottom of the notch. Holding it vertically, grasp the tab firmly and pull. The entire leather piece will spin as the correct size of stripping is cut. It is amazing how many feet of lacing can be produced from an 8-inch circle.

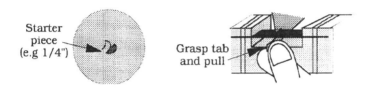

Starter
piece
(e.g 1/4")

Grasp tab
and pull

Jig. You will need to construct a form (jig) for bending the shoes. In the interest of time, and should you be willing to spend the money, you can make two of the forms. The instructions are for one.

Before you begin, you will need to determine the proper size snowshoe based on your weight:

Up to 125 pounds	9 inches x 42 inches
126 to 150 pounds	10 inches x 48 inches
151 to 200 pounds	10 inches x 56 inches
Over 200 pounds	11 inches x 56-58 inches

Our instructions are for 10 inches by 56 inches.

To make your jig, you will need a plank. Get a board(s) equal in width and length to the size shoes you will build and at least 2 inches thick. If you use more than one board to achieve the required width, they will need to be cut to dimension and fastened together. You can do this with a biscuit router and glued inserts, by flat brackets, or by any other method that does not interfere with the bending of the shoes. The board(s) may be of hard or soft wood; soft wood, such as pine or hem fir, costs less.

Round off one end of the plank. You can use a rasp or power sander for this. Be sure the finished surface is smooth to the touch and fairly even from side to side. Begin the rounding 3 to 4 inches back from the end of the board, depending on how severe you want the front turn-up to be.

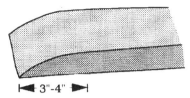

You need two pieces of hardwood; they should be 1/2 inch longer than the width of the shoe (for ours, 10 1/2 inches and 8 inches), 1 3/4 inches wide, and 1 inch thick – they will attach to the jig as spreaders. Cut the two hardwood pieces as shown:

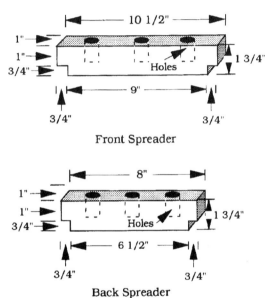

Front Spreader

Back Spreader

Attach the spreaders securely to the plank. One way is to drill holes in the top and screw from the holes into the board below. The location of the spreaders will vary with the size of the shoe. For ours (10 x 56 inches), put one 11 inches from bottom of the rounded end to the front of the spreader, the other 27 1/2 inches from the rounding to the front of the spreader. Center both spreaders on the width of the board.

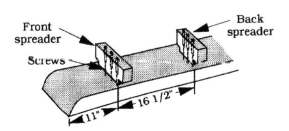

Lastly, take a sturdy board (at least 1 x 6 x 12 inches) and make a rectangular hole 4 inches from one end and centered across the width. Make the hole 1 inch across and 3/4 inch long.

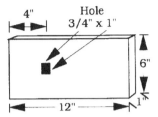

Screw or nail the board to the underside of the rounded end of the jig. It should be centered (across the width) on the plank; the hole should be exactly abutted to the end of the plank.

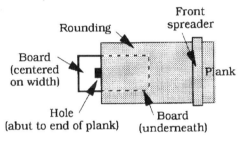

The frame (outside) of the snowshoe has to be bent. This means that if you want to *buy* the wood for it, you should get a premium wood, such as straight-grained ash, from a lumberyard. It will be dry so you need to steam or treat it in boiling water to make it limber enough to bend. Buying wood is the easiest in the long run. But if that is your decision, keep in mind that, when the wood is prepared and ready for bending, you will have about two minutes in which to complete the task before the wood becomes too cool and unpliable to work.

There are two other sources for frame wood. One is to find a place where you can cut a tree or some saplings of hardwood, such as elm, ash, spruce, birch, maple, or any other hardwood except oak. Oak will not do the job – *do not succumb to the temptation to use it.* If you have no other choices, willow can work if you can find some that is straight and without knots.

To use saplings, you must find two that are long enough for your needs, of about an equal diameter (1 1/2 to 1 3/4 inches, end to end), and without any knots. Be sure the saplings are green, not cured on the stump.

If you choose a live tree, it should have an 8- to 9-inch diameter at the base and be straight and free of limbs and knots at least for the length of your shoes. Use the sapwood – the wood lying just under the bark. The heartwood won't work. Once the tree is on the ground, saw out the section you selected and split the tree into halves, quarters, then if possible into eighths. The wood you choose, when finished, should have grain that runs straight for its entire length; anything else may break during bending, so judge accordingly.

Much of the shaping can be done for you at a sawmill. If you choose to do it yourself, work the two best pieces (or saplings) with a draw–shave, knife, or saw while the wood is fresh. The two frame pieces should be 3/4 x 3/4 inch at the mid-center and taper to 1/2 x 1/2 inch at the ends. Put a slight chamfer on all edges.

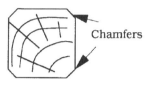

Chamfers

BENDING AND SHAPING THE SHOES

While the frame pieces are still green and pliable or hot from steam or water, poke one end of each through the hole in the front end of the jig. Align the frame ends evenly, allowing about 3 inches (or to your taste) to protrude below the hole. Clamp the front ends together to hold them securely in position.

Drive a V-shaped wedge (about 1 1/2 x 3/4 inches) between the two frame pieces to spread them. The size of the wedge depends on the size of the shoe – the perfect wedge will remain tight when the frames are bent into the spreaders.

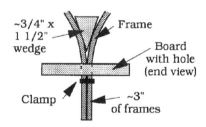

~3/4" x 1 1/2" wedge

Frame

Board with hole (end view)

Clamp

~3" of frames

Slowly bend both frame pieces down until they will slip under the first spreader. If the wood resists to the point you fear it will break, you can treat it with steam or boiling water. You also may heat it with a torch, but proceed very slowly! Using a torch means lots of sanding later. If the wood twists as you bend it, you are forcing it. Slow down!

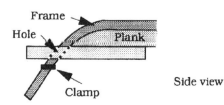

Frame

Hole

Plank

Clamp

Side view

When the frame pieces are under the first (front) spreader, pull the tail ends together, letting them slip under the second (back) spreader. Clamp or tie the tails together 6 inches from the ends. Let the frames dry in the jig for at least a week.

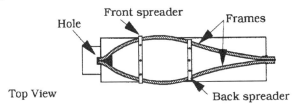

To make the permanent crossbars, measure 17 1/2 inches on both frames from the back end of the shoe; this will be the *front* of the *back* crossbar. From that point, measure 22 inches forward on both sides; this will be the *front* of the *front* crossbar.

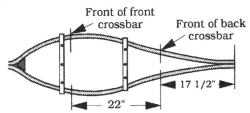

Now measure across each shoe between the corresponding marks, front and back, at both crossbar locations.

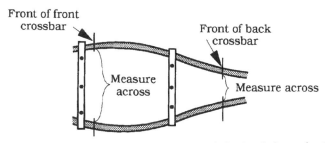

Measure 1 3/8 inches along the frame toward the back from the front of the crossbar markers. This will be the back of the crossbars. Measure the distances across the shoe at those points.

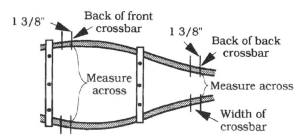

Cut two crossbars from hardwood. The length of each is the measurements you have made + 1/2 inch (which allows a 1/4-inch tenon on each side of the frame); hence they will be cut to follow the taper of the bent frame. The boards should be 5/16-inch thick and 1 3/8-inches wide.

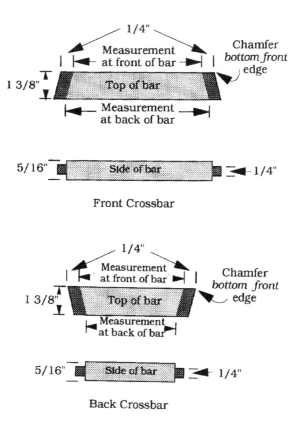

Front Crossbar

Back Crossbar

Tie or put a temporary clamp on the front end of the shoe just above where the tips go into the hole in the jig. Remove the spreaders and take the frames off the jig.

Wrap the front and rear ends with wet rawhide. There are two methods for this. For the front, simply wrap rawhide around the ends, tucking the ends of the rawhide under.

At the tail, drill three or more holes centered down the tips of the shoe frame. Lace through the holes, crossing the lacing on top like a street shoe, and tuck in or tie off the ends.

Lacing

Let the rawhide dry and remove the clamps.

On the inside of the frame pieces between your marks for crossbars, cut mortises 1/4 inch deep. A router, chisel, or drill press (or a combination) may be used. Insert the tenons of the crossbars into the mortises, trimming as needed for a close fit. This step will need a lot of patience.

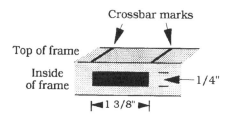

Drill holes, perpendicular to the frames, in the crossbars and in the sides as shown in **Figures 1 and 2.** Locations are approximate because they will vary slightly depending on the size shoes you are building. Webbing between either end of the shoe and the nearest crossbar will be 1/8-inch lacing or rawhide; holes may be 1/8 inch to 3/16 inch.

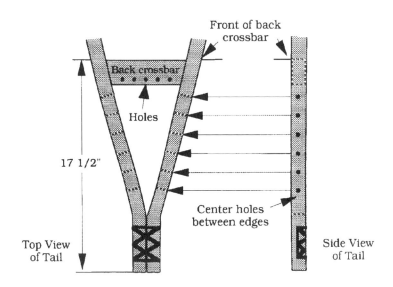

Figure 1. Drilling Holes in Frame Tail and Back Crossbar

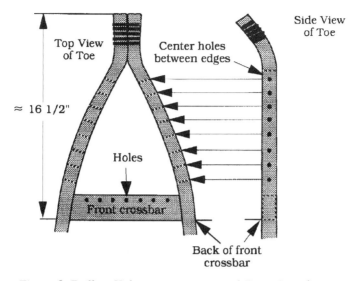

Figure 2. Drilling Holes in Frame Toe and Front Crossbar

When the holes in the toe and tail sections are drilled, sand the shoes to a fine finish. Inspect your work for any remaining details that need completion and pat yourself on the back for a job well done so far!

WEAVING THE WEBBING

Weaving will be easier if you make a shuttle to help in pulling the lacing over and under. A simple shuttle can be made from a thin (1/8 inch), oblong piece of wood about 3 inches x 1/2 inch. Starting from near the middle of the piece of wood, round it down to very thin edges on both sides all the way around. Drill a hole in the middle large enough to thread the lacing through easily. Sand the shuttle with fine sandpaper to ensure a very smooth surface. Thread the lacing through and tie a knot in the end so it stays put while you weave.

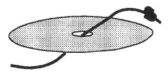

You also need a spring clamp handy to hold the lacing taut if you take a break during the weaving process (a near certainty). If you find the lacing loosening up while you weave, use the clamp. It provides that third hand you always wished you had. It is easy to miss a step. Keep in mind that in weaving the webbing, *it is always over one, under one*. If you discover you've missed one, tear out what you've done back to the missed step and fix it.

Soak your rawhide strips thoroughly before you use them. Stretch them as much as you can, but don't reduce their width too much.

During the process, you will need to splice your rawhide strips. Do this as shown below, pulling them together tightly.

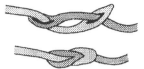

Lace the toe and tail sections first. The toe takes about 12 feet of 1/8-inch lacing; the tail, about 6 feet. It is easier to weave if you sit in a chair with the opposite end underneath you. Sitting on the shoe holds it in place, keeps it out of the way, and puts you close over your work. Snug the rawhide tightly, but don't overdo it. If you do, it can pull the frame out of alignment when it dries. Follow the illustrations shown in **Figures 3 and 4.**

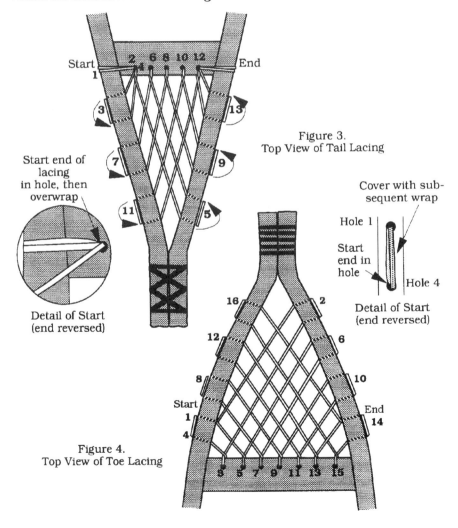

Start

Start end of lacing in hole, then overwrap

Figure 3.
Top View of Tail Lacing

Cover with subsequent wrap

Hole 1

Start end in hole

Hole 4

Detail of Start
(end reversed)

Detail of Start
(end reversed)

Figure 4.
Top View of Toe Lacing

For the middle webbing, you need about 28 feet of 1/4-inch lacing or rawhide. Space and mark where you want to fasten the webbing to the frame sides.

At the tail end marks (3 3/4 inches up from the back crossbar), wrap a piece of rawhide twice around the frame, bring it across the top and wrap it twice around the other side of the frame, tucking in the end tightly.

At the toe end marks (3 1/2 inches back from the front crossbar), tuck the starting end under and, going underneath first, wrap across and back twice; this forms the four-strand master cord. Weave the pattern, under and over, using the shuttle where it is helpful, following the numbers. This will provide the white lacing pattern in the illustration (**Figure 5**).

Pay particular attention to spacing. Don't let the knots slip; if they do fix them immediately. It's impossible to correct them later. Also take care not to pull the webbing so tight that the master cord or the horizontal lacing across the back is pulled out of alignment. *Keep them tight, but straight, during assembly!*

When the numbered (white) webbing is completed, the lettered webbing is woven through. It is shaded in the illustration; it may be dyed to add decoration. Fasten it where shown at (a) and follow the alphabetical order, finally fastening off at (h). The master cord may want to bend. Don't let it.

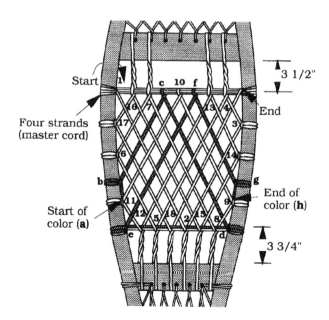

Figure 5. Top View of Middle Section Lacing

Twist strands that go over the crossbars. Either of the two knots below may be used to anchor the lacing to the sides of the frame:

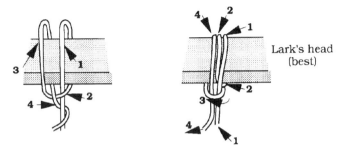

Lark's head
(best)

After you complete the webbing, set the shoe aside to dry. When drying is complete, give the entire shoe, webbing and all, three successive coats of spar varnish, letting each coat dry thoroughly before applying the next coat.

BINDINGS

Two bindings are described — with and without an instep strap (**Figures 6 and 7**, respectively). If you want the strap, the toe piece is laced through holes in its side and tied to the master cord. If there is no instep strap, the heel strap is threaded through the toe piece and under the master cord.

Once you've decided which binding to use, lay out the toe piece pattern and cut out the leather. Measure and cut the straps to the lengths you need and assemble the binding. Use either rivets or rawhide to hold the buckles in place. Attach the binding to the master cord, adjusting it so that your boot toe will clear the crossbar by at least 1/2 inch.

It is better to have straps a little too long than too short. Keep all buckles to the outside of the foot. Put on a boot the size you will wear when using the snowshoes and lace the toe piece over it. Don't make it so tight that you have to retie it each time you use it. When this is done, you are ready to go. Enjoy your new shoes!

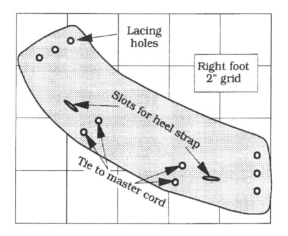

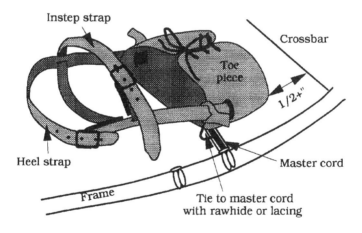

Figure 6. Binding with Instep Strap

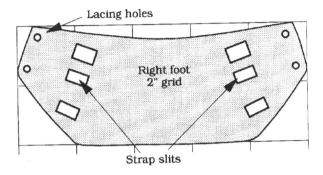

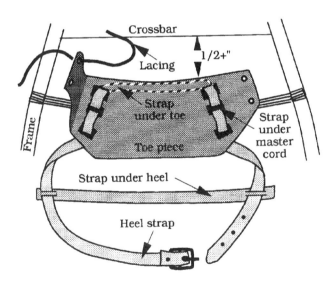

Figure 7. Binding without Instep Strap

MAKING
POMMEL
BAGS

MAKING POMMEL BAGS

Most pommel bags sold in tack shops or advertised in horse magazines share a unique phenomenon. People buy them, try them, then hang them in the tack room and leave them there. Why? Because they ride on the sides of the pommel, they are made of stiff leather and designed to lie flat so they don't interfere with the rider's legs. That means they cannot carry much cargo. Secondly, they flop around at any gait above a walk if enough is stored in them to make them bulge. When they flop, gear can be lost. Most fit only a limited range of saddle horn sizes and they cost a lot. There are other disadvantages, but you get the idea.

The pommel bags shown here eliminate most problems. They can be made to lie flat and will not flop around even when stuffed full. They are large enough to carry a roll of toilet paper on one side and binoculars and/or lunch on the other, but are still out of the way of the rider's legs. They can be secured so they do not lose their contents. They can be tailored to fit any size horn and cost little to make. The pattern can be modified, e.g., outside pockets, divided pouches, to accommodate special needs or preferences.

MATERIALS

Heavy garment-tanned leather for bags, one piece at least 36 inches long (lengthwise of grain). A piece 36 inches long and 24 inches wide will accommodate all pieces easily

Piece of pigskin 8 inches square

14 feet of 1/4-inch latigo leather

One 3/4-inch buckle, two 1/2-inch buckles

Two wheel-weights (local garage) or saltwater fishing weights (sporting goods store)

Artificial sinew or linen thread

If you're sewing by hand, a three-cornered glover's needle or veterinary needle

Just about any supple leather can be used to make the bags, but fairly heavy garment-tanned leather (like that used for chaps) from elk, buffalo, or cow is recommended. Stiff leather, such as latigo, will not work for the bag itself, but is preferred for the straps. Pigskin is best for the trim around the saddle horn opening because it won't stretch out over time. Nearly any style buckle will work, but flat ones with center attach points are best; they can be purchased at most tack shops or hardware stores.

The bags can be sewn by hand or by machine. (A shoe repair shop often will sew them for you at a reasonable price.) If you're sewing by hand, use a three-cornered glover's needle or veterinary needle; the holes they make will not tear out or stretch like the holes made from round needles. Artificial sinew for thread, split three or four times, is very strong and does not rot. Several strands of linen thread will also work.

The hearts on the bag flaps are not mere decoration. They hold lead weights that make the flaps fall into place in case you are in a hurry and forget to tie them down. The lead can be made by hammering flat a wheel-weight or saltwater fishing weight.

The latigo thongs attached to the end tabs of the bag back are for tying the bags to a D-ring or saddle latigo strings. They hold the bags firmly in place, which is especially handy when you're riding in brushy terrain.

LAYING OUT THE PATTERN AND CUTTING OUT THE PIECES

You may want to lay out the pattern on heavy paper, then transfer it to your leather. That way you have it for future use without remeasuring. Draw the pattern pieces as shown in **Figures 1 and 2.** Mark lines A-B and A'-B' 12 inches from the ends of the tabs. Cut out the pattern pieces and lay them on your leather, lengthwise of the grain. Trace around them with a soft pencil, marking lines A-B and A'-B'. Cut 1/2-inch-wide welting strips from the scrap pile.

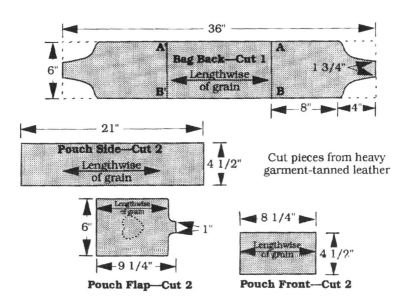

Figure 1. Bag Pattern Pieces

Cut 2 of each
from latigo leather

Figure 2. Buckle Straps for Pouch Flap Closure

ASSEMBLING THE POMMEL BAGS

Sew all seams with an in-and-out running stitch. Make each stitch about 1/8 inch long and about 1/8 inch apart, overstitching every few stitches to lock them in place. Put a piece of welting between the layers of the bag for all seams. Use 1/4-inch seam allowances.

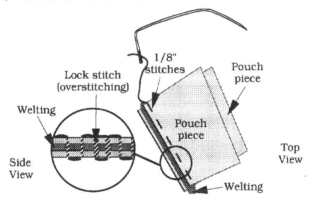

Sewing Pouch Fronts to Pouch Sides. Attach the buckle straps to the pouch fronts. First cut an elongated hole in the center of each 4 1/2-inch strap. Place the tang through the hole. Double the straps and center them 1/2 inch from the bottom of the pouch fronts. Sew straps to pouch fronts with running stitches.

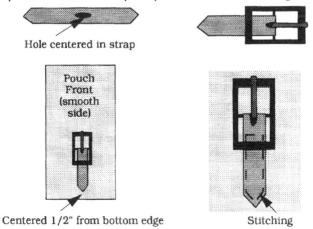

Each pouch side "wraps around" the two long sides and the buckled short side of the front. Place welting between the smooth (grain) side of the front and side pieces. The grain side will be outside on the finished pouch, the seam to the inside. Sew the pouch fronts to the pouch sides with a 1/4-inch seam allowance. Turn pouches right side out (grain side to the front).

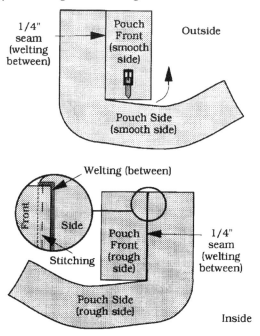

Sewing Pouches to Bag Back. Place one pocket on the bag back. Put the rough side of the pocket against the *smooth* (grain) side of the back. Align the top of the pocket with line A-B. Put welting in the seam all the way around; ease the fullness of the side at the corners (4 inches from the end of the back). Sew a 1/4-inch seam with running stitches through all thicknesses around the pocket, putting a lock stitch every few stitches. Repeat these steps for the second pocket along line A'-B'.

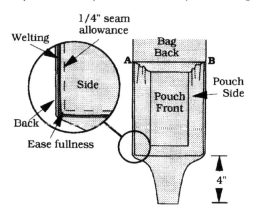

Sewing Pouch Flaps to Bag Back. Hammer your lead weights until they are flat. Smooth side down, center the heart-shaped buckle-strap piece horizontally and vertically on the rough side of the pouch flap. Insert a lead piece between the flap and the strap. On the smooth side, sew around the heart and through the buckle strap on the wrong side, enclosing the lead between the two layers. On the right side, the heart becomes decorative, so try to keep your stitches even. Punch holes about 3/4 inch apart up the length of the strap.

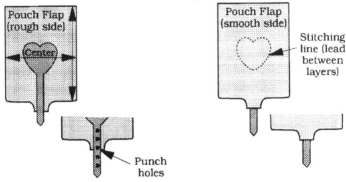

Next attach the pocket flaps to the back (**Figure 3**). Place each flap, *rough side up,* on top of the bag back. Align the short straight end of the flap along line A-B (or A′-B′) with the tabbed end *away* from the pocket. Put welting between the back and the flap and sew the flap to the back with 1/8-inch running stitches (and occasional lock stitches) through all thicknesses.

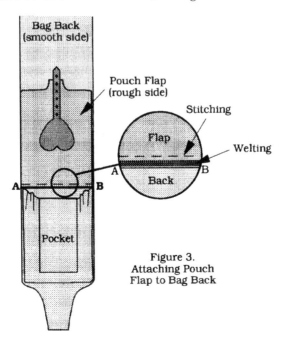

Figure 3.
Attaching Pouch
Flap to Bag Back

Trim all welting next to the stitching line, but be careful not to cut any stitches. Fold the flaps over and buckle them to keep them out of the way.

MAKING THE SADDLE HORN HOLE

Measure around the smallest saddle horn you plan to use (circumference). Take your measurement below the top at the narrowest part of the horn. The saddle horn hole is adjustable for about 3 inches. If you ride a saddle with a very large horn, it will probably not fit if you measure a very small horn. Think about how adaptable your bags need to be and choose your circumference accordingly. Divide your circumference measure by 3.14 to get the diameter. Draw a circle with 1/2 the diameter (radius) as the center and make a pattern. Place your pattern with the center point halfway between lines A-B and A'-B' and the edge of the circle against one side of the bag back.

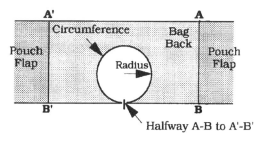

Cut a piece of pigskin to fit around the hole for reinforcing. Make the inside diameter the diameter of the pattern and the outside diameter 1 inch wider all the way around. Sew the pigskin to the hole, trimming it evenly along the bag back.

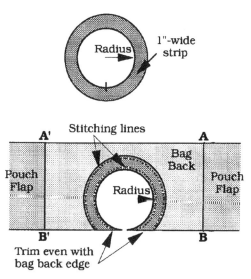

Cut two contoured 1/2-inch-wide strips of latigo leather. Make one 3 1/2 inches long, the other 8 inches long.

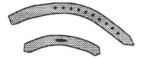

In the 3 1/2-inch strip, cut a centered elongated hole. Insert the tang of a 1/2-inch buckle and double the strap over it. Sew the strap to one side of the horn hole, back about 1 inch from the point of the reinforcing pigskin. Punch holes in the 8-inch strap about 1/2-inch apart for about 5 inches from one end. Sew the other end to the opposite side of the horn hole, starting about 1 inch back from the point of the reinforcement.

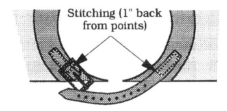

Stitching (1" back from points)

FINISHING THE POMMEL BAGS

Cut four reinforcing pieces of pigskin for the tab ends of the bag back and the pouch flaps. Sew them in place. Punch two holes in the pouch flap tab; cut a 3/8-inch hole in the tab of the bag back. Cut two latigo strings 36 inches long. Put one through each hole in the bag back tabs; these are used to tie the bag to a D-ring or saddle ties to keep the bags from flopping around. The holes in the pouch flaps can be used to tie down the flaps.

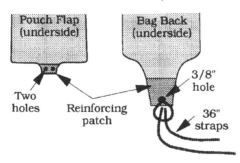

Pouch Flap (underside)

Bag Back (underside)

Two holes

Reinforcing patch

3/8" hole

36" straps

Punch twelve holes in the top of each pouch about 3/4 inch down from the top. The holes should be spaced six on each side as follows:

One near the seam joining the pouch front and pouch side
Four equally spaced across the pouch side
One near the seam joining the pouch side and bag back

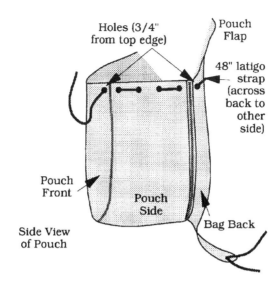

Holes (3/4"
from top edge)

Pouch
Flap

48" latigo
strap
(across
back to
other
side)

Pouch
Front

Pouch
Side

Bag Back

Side View
of Pouch

Cut two 48-inch latigo thongs and thread them through the holes in the pouches; bring the ends out through the holes in the pouch fronts and across the bag backs on the outside. The thongs can be pulled tightly and tied to prevent things from falling out of the pouches. The pouch buckles and straps can secure the contents even when the pouches are relatively empty.

MAKING
RAWHIDE

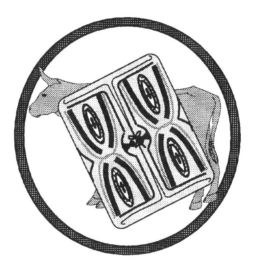

MAKING RAWHIDE

Rawhide is a very versatile material. Because it stretches when wet and shrinks while drying, it is useful for binding things together. To date, it is unsurpassed for making snowshoes and Indian drum heads. Tool handles, such as rakes, shovels, hatchets and hoes, can be sturdily repaired with it. Moccasins can be soled with rawhide, and it is good for a variety of patching and reinforcing tasks.

In the wilderness, in emergency or survival conditions, making rawhide may be as simple as shaping something out of a green hide with the hair still on, letting it dry, and using it. Singeing the hair off in the flames of a fire and cutting some of the hide into laces and using them with the rest of the hide to make crude moccasins or snowshoes is possible. But in the comfort of home, rawhide-making can be more convenient.

MATERIALS

Hide
Large plastic or stainless steel tub (or line a metal tub with a plastic
    garbage bag)
Lime or lye (if you want to remove hair chemically)
Fleshing beam (p. 114) or large plastic pipe
2x6s for frame (if you want to use one)
Nylon cord, leather lacings, or tacks for stretching the hide
Edged tool, such as a blunt knife or draw-shave, for scraping
Rock, hammer, or pole ax if you want lofty rawhide

CLEANING THE HIDE

Other than donating them to the Boy Scouts, making rawhide is perhaps the easiest thing you can do with animal skins. Rawhide can be made from any pelt or hide, but cow, elk, or deer is best. If you have a large hide, such as cow or elk, you will discover that it is very heavy and bulky. In such cases, you'll want to split the hide down the middle for ease of handling and processing. If the hide still has the leg extensions, cut them off to square up the hide. The few inches of rawhide you gain by leaving them on is not worth the effort it takes to handle the dangling appendages.

Whatever hide is used, it should be prepared as carefully as if you were going to tan it. There are several methods to hold the hide while you clean it: peg it out on the ground, drape it over a log, tack it on a barn or shed wall, lace it into a frame.

The first step is to wash away any blood and dirt. Pick off large pieces of fat and tissue and any adhering debris. Use soap and warm water and a stiff scrub brush to really work the flesh side over. Get it as clean as you can. Once finished, you can let the hide dry until it is flint-hard and stack it away for future processing or move right along to complete the job.

DEHAIRING THE HIDE

In ancient times, American Indians approached the task of dehairing hides by scraping the hair and scarf-skin off with stone and bone tools. The scarf-skin is the thin, nearly cellophane-like tissue that lies just under the hair or, on the flesh side, under the flesh. To make the task easier, the Indians either soaked the hides in water or a mixture of water and wood ashes until the hair "slipped" (began to fall out), or they buried the skin in moist earth until they achieved the same effect. There are quicker and more effective methods available today.

In all forms of leather processing, it is best not to let the hide come in contact with base metal other than scraping tools. For soaking, either use plastic or stainless steel vessels or line metal buckets and cans with plastic bags. An old washing machine tub works well.

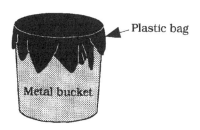

Plastic bag

Metal bucket

One method of getting the hair to "slip" — that is, become loose enough that it is easily removed — is to soak it in a lime solution. Mix 2 quarts of hydrated lime (usually available at a farm supply store) with 10 gallons of unchlorinated water. Let the mixture stand for at least an hour. If the hide you are going to process is dry and stiff, wet it until it is supple. Stir the lime solution and, being careful not to get the liquid on you, insert the hide. Let it stand for five days to two weeks or until the hair comes off with only light pulling. During this time you will want to stir the hide around with a stick occasionally to ensure all surfaces are exposed and thoroughly soaked with solution.

A faster method to remove the hair is to soak it for eight to fourteen hours in a water/lye solution. Mix 2 tablespoons of lye (Red Devil brand is very good) with enough water to cover the hide by about 2 inches. This is where an old washer comes in handy, especially if it will still agitate. Using a stick, submerge the hide and really work it around to be sure it is thoroughly soaked. Be careful not to splash the liquid on your clothes or skin. Unless you have an old washer that agitates, whenever you think of it, go back and stir the hide some more. Use rubber gloves if you are going to test the hair for slippage. Usually you will go to bed while the hide is still soaking. By the time you get up, much of the hair will fall out as you handle the hide.

Whichever method you use, when the hair slips easily, remove the hide from solution. Remember, use a stick or, if you insist on using your hands, wear rubber gloves that don't leak. Rinse the hide in three successive changes of clear water. Be sure to stir it around well to get all the lime or lye out of it. When you are certain you have the skin properly rinsed, do it one more time. Remove the hide from the rinse and wring it out. Use all the energy you can muster. You may even find a friend to make the task easier.

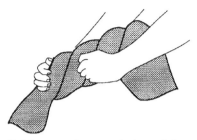

Now you have to finish removing any hair and the scarf-skin on both sides of the hide. You can place the hide on a fleshing beam, a frame, even a barn door to stabilize it while you scrape.

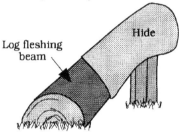

If you want to use a frame, it should be constructed of something as sturdy as 2x6s. The frame has to be strong (corner braces are a plus) and large enough to allow at least a free 6 to 12 inches of space all the way around the largest hide you will work in it. You can use 3-inch staples for lacing pins or even nails driven into the outer edges of the boards. Space them proportionally the same distance apart as you will make the lacing holes in the hides you will work. Remember — the hide will stretch while it is being processed. Punch lacing holes at least 1/4 inch inside the edge of the hide from 4 to 6 inches apart, depending on the spacing you used on the frame.

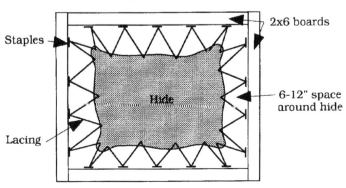

Traditionalists will use leather or cord lacings, but for those who like a forgiving, no-hassle tool, nylon parachute cord is the material of choice for lacing the hide to the frame. It can be untied in cold weather and has enough give to prevent "blowouts" or tearing.

If you use a wall or barn door, tack the hide on, beginning in the center of one edge and alternating with the other. Space the tacks about 4 to 6 inches apart. Pull the hide firmly as you go, but don't stretch it. When you finish the sides, do the top and bottom the same way.

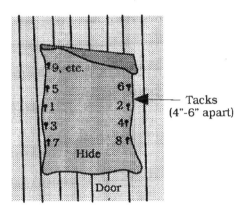

The actual dehairing can be done with any edged tool, such as the edge of a paddle, an animal shoulder bone, the spine of a knife, or a draw-shave. Work the hide until all the hair has been removed. If the hair does not come off readily, return it to the soaking solution for another cycle.

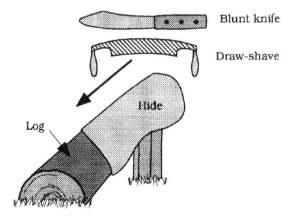

Once the hair is off, scrape the hide with a knife edge, hoe blade, or draw-shave until the scarf-skin is all removed. This is work! But keep at it until it is done. The tools shouldn't be sharp because, if they are, you must be careful not to cut the hide. Do not let the hide dry completely while you are working it. If necessary, stop and re-wet it enough to keep it pliable.

When you have finished the hair side, turn the hide over and scrape the flesh side until all vestiges of debris and scarf-skin are gone from that side. Rinse the hide one more time to make sure all the chemicals are removed.

Now you have to decide what kind of rawhide you want. If you will be satisfied with flint-hard rawhide that makes good drum heads, reinforcements, snowshoe laces and such, lay your hide out and let it dry. You're done until you want it for a specific application.

If, however, you want white, lofty material that will make beautiful parfleches, moccasin soles, backing, belts, equipment laces, or slings, there is work yet to be done. One benefit of this kind of rawhide is that, if you missed any scarf-skin, it will be removed in the final process.

LOFTING THE RAWHIDE

You can do the next step on concrete that is large enough to work the hide on, but if you have a frame, it will prove its worth. Keep the hide only slightly damp. Use a fist-size rock (early Indians did) or a hammer or the blunt end of a pole ax. Begin overstriking the hide. Move across the hide from one side to the other in a straight line. Repeat until the entire hide has been covered by your skidding overstrikes, which can be seen as wavy parallel lines on the surface of the hide.

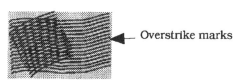 ◄— Overstrike marks

The object is to break the fibers, creating "loft." Your success will be apparent as the hide gets thicker and turns white. If, when you have gone over the entire hide, it is not as lofty and white as you believe it should be, do it again . . . and again, if necessary.

If you are not using a frame, use a concrete pad such as a driveway. The same process as above applies and, while rocks and hammers will do the job, the ax head works best and fastest on concrete as long as the muscles above your kidneys and in your wrists and forearms hold out.

Rawhides can be stored for extended periods of time. Should you wish, you can soak them until they are pliable and then tan them into leather. Rawhide is not only useful but, compared to tanned leather, it also is quickly processed and any excess can be readily sold or traded.

MAKING RAWHIDE SADDLE STIRRUPS

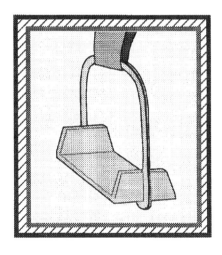

MAKING RAWHIDE SADDLE STIRRUPS

Rawhide stirrups — more accurately, rawhide-*covered* stirrups — look good, are inexpensive to make, and are historically correct for the periods before, during, and after the fur trade in American history.

As with many projects, the tools for making and covering the stirrups can be as simple as a pocketknife, hand saw, awl, and cord or thread. They may be as elaborate as those in a full-scale workshop. Stirrups may be fashioned in an emergency on the trail in survival circumstances or in a couple of leisure hours in the friendly environment of your den. The methods are flexible.

The style of stirrup depends on your taste and available materials. The early Spaniards in America often used hand-carved, one-piece stirrups; the Indians usually assembled several small pieces of wood. The style described here follows the Indian practice.

There are several ways of making a stirrup that will be functional and long-wearing. For simplicity only one is described, but materials and shape can be adapted to suit your tastes.

MATERIALS

For each stirrup, you will need:

A wooden rod, 3/8-inch to 1/2-inch in diameter x 19 1/2 inches long
    or a 3/8-inch iron rod about 18 1/2 inches long
A piece of wood that will finish to a size of 5 inches x 3 inches x
    1/2 inch. Hardwood is desirable, but the Indians often used cotton-
    wood and it worked
Two pieces of wood 3 inches x 1 1/2 inches x 3/8 inch
Tacks, pegs, and/or screws (carpet tacks are not good because they
    rust easily)
Presoaked rawhide — enough for two pieces, each about 8 inches by
    22 inches (20 inches should be enough unless you don't pull your
    rawhide tight)
Artificial sinew or thin strips of rawhide lacing
Needles (curved veterinary needles work especially well)

Spray bottle of water (to keep rawhide wet as you work it)
Small *sturdy* spring clamps
Pliers to pull and stretch rawhide over wood corners
Shellac or beeswax

The wooden rod for the stirrup bow should be green and knot-free. If it is not green, you will have to soak, steam, or boil it to make it supple enough to bend. Depending on your final goal, any wood may be used; willow, alder, or elm all can be good choices. The American Indians generally used cottonwood. Once iron became common, they sometimes used metal rod. You can do the same if you wish, although the process will vary slightly from the one for wood.

Rawhide is relatively simple to make. For those who'd like to do that, refer to the chapter on *Making Rawhide*. Ready-made rawhide can be obtained from suppliers listed in the back of this book.

If you are in a hurry or want a real challenge, go to your local supermarket and buy a bag of rawhide dog bones. The bones come in two varieties: those that are made from one large piece (about one foot square) and those that are made from two or more small pieces twisted together. Only luck and experience will help you with selection. Soak your dog bones until they can be unwound and are soft enough to be worked. Pieces can be sewn together to make a piece large enough for the stirrup, or they may be wrapped onto the stirrup individually and sewn together in place. One piece of rawhide for each stirrup makes work easier, however.

MAKING THE STIRRUP

The wood pieces for one stirrup are illustrated below:

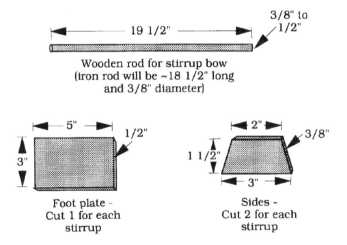

19 1/2"

3/8" to 1/2"

Wooden rod for stirrup bow
(iron rod will be ~18 1/2" long
and 3/8" diameter)

5"   1/2"   3"

Foot plate -
Cut 1 for each
stirrup

2"   3/8"   1 1/2"   3"

Sides -
Cut 2 for each
stirrup

Cut out the wood pieces. If you want a different shape to the side pieces, cut them to the shape you desire. (More corners may mean more pulling and tugging to make the rawhide tight, but many shapes can be done.)

If you're using a wooden rod, cut it into two pieces, one 14 1/2 inches, the other 5 inches. If the piece is green, strip the bark from it. If you are using cured wood, soak or steam or boil the 14 1/2-inch piece until it is supple enough to bend without breaking or splintering.

Using something round (plastic PVC pipe or a coffee can works well) with about a 4-inch diameter as a mandrel, bend the wood to shape. The result should have a 5-inch internal diameter at the top and a 5-inch span at the bottom. Tie the rod in place and let it dry until it will retain the new shape.

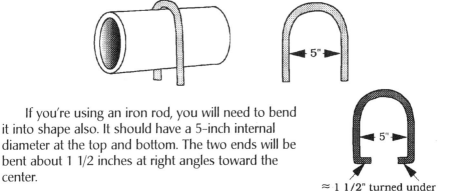

If you're using an iron rod, you will need to bend it into shape also. It should have a 5-inch internal diameter at the top and bottom. The two ends will be bent about 1 1/2 inches at right angles toward the center.

≈ 1 1/2" turned under

ASSEMBLING THE STIRRUP

It's best to peg or tack the wood pieces together initially. The stirrup can be assembled without securing them before you put on the rawhide, but it makes that job *much* more difficult and the stirrup less durable.

> *Drill holes before you put in pegs, tacks, or screws.*
> *If you don't, the wood will split.*

To peg the pieces together, drill the holes the size of the pegs (which must be smaller than the rods), put some glue in the hole, and place the peg. Smooth the ends of the peg so they are flush with the outside surfaces. If you use screws, countersink them.

For a wood bow. First center the 5-inch rod on the bottom of the foot plate. Drill two holes (at least 1 inch from the ends) through the rod into the plate, but do not go entirely through the plate! Put in the pegs, tacks, or screws.

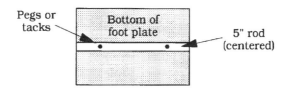

Place the two side pieces on top of the foot plate, aligning them with the edges of the plate. Drill two holes in the bottom through the plate into the sides and secure them. Sand the foot plate and sides until smooth and round all corners and edges slightly.

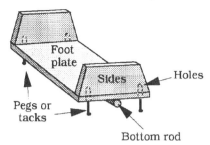

Attach the wood stirrup bow with two pegs or tacks. It should line up with the rod underneath, centered on the side pieces, and be pegged to both.

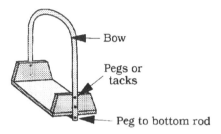

For an iron bow. Secure the sides to the foot plate first. Sand the foot plate and sides smooth and round all corners and edges slightly.

Center the rod on the ends of the foot plate with the turned-under ends beneath the plate. Drill two holes through the rod, and into, but not through, the sides. Drill two more holes on the bent-under part of the rod, one near the bend and one at the end, and into the foot plate. Countersink all holes. Put in four screws on each side.

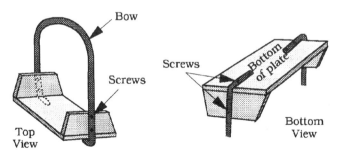

GENERAL INSTRUCTIONS FOR WRAPPING AND SEWING THE RAWHIDE

The seam will go across the center of the underneath side of the foot plate, up the center of the outside of the side pieces, and across the top of the bow. You will work from the bottom of the plate, up the sides and across the bow to its top where the rawhide ends finally will be joined.

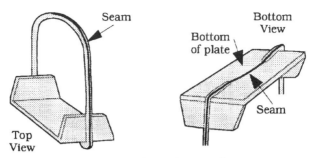

You must trim the rawhide carefully and in small increments as you work it into shape over the wood and sew it into place.

Although the rawhide ends sometimes can be very cumbersome, resist the temptation to trim anything beyond the very restricted area you are working on – and trim that in very narrow pieces.

Sew the seam with baseball stitches (best) or with overcast stitches. A running stitch that creates a lip ridge of rawhide is not good for at least two reasons: as it dries, the seam may tend to separate and the ridge can become sharp enough to give you a bad cut.

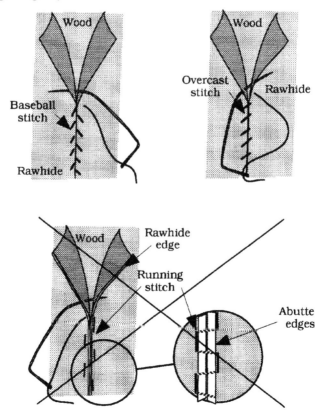

You can sew the rawhide as shown by using a needle and artificial sinew or you can punch holes with an awl and lace the edges together with thin strips of wet rawhide. During the sewing or lacing, pull firmly enough to draw the edges tightly together, but not overlapping. If you're sewing so tightly that the holes begin to stretch, take a stitch next to where the needle just came out before going back across the seam. It will help to take the strain off the hole so the stitching will not pull out.

WRAPPING THE STIRRUP WITH RAWHIDE

For a one-piece application, lay out the rawhide and cut a piece about 8 inches by 20 to 22 inches for each stirrup.

Mark the center of the rawhide piece lengthwise and crosswise. Also mark the center of the foot plate in both directions. Place the rawhide *on the top of the foot plate inside the bow,* matching the centers, with the lengthwise direction going up the bow. For the next step, it may help to put tacks into the rawhide and wood where the sides and bottom join on the inside of the stirrup.

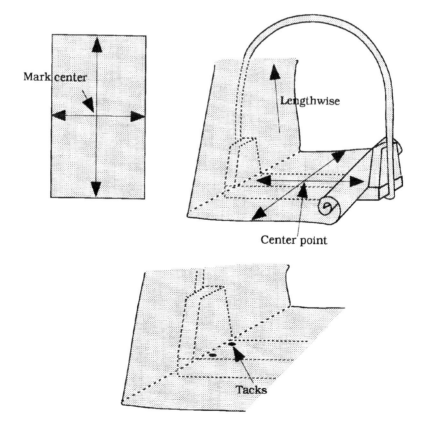

Mark center

Lengthwise

Center point

Tacks

Stretch the rawhide snugly widthwise around the plate. On the bottom side, trim carefully to allow a gap of about 3/8 inch between the edges; trim both edges equally and ensure the rawhide stays centered across the foot plate. So far this has been the easy part!

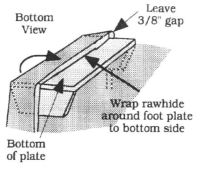

Bottom
View

Leave
3/8" gap

Wrap rawhide
around foot plate
to bottom side

Bottom
of plate

Sew the two edges of the rawhide together across the bottom of the foot plate and rod. As you sew, work and stretch the rawhide so the edges abut as you pull the stitches tight; at the ends of the stitching, pull and stretch the rawhide so it goes over the corners of the foot plate and up the sides. It may help to begin sewing in the middle and go to one edge, then begin in the middle again and sew to the other edge. Make the stitches about 1/4 inch apart.

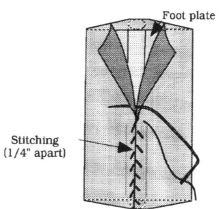

Foot plate

Stitching
(1/4" apart)

The job is about to get more difficult. Turn the stirrup over. You now have a problem. The rawhide is bunched up at the inside corners of the foot plate. This is the tricky part throughout the wrapping. Using pliers, your fingers, whatever works for you, stretch the outside and work the lumps out of the inside until you have a smooth groove across the junction of the bottom and sides of the stirrup. It takes patience and some hard tugging. Use your spray bottle of water to keep the rawhide wet – stretching will dry it out – or resoak it as necessary. Keep at it until you have worked out all the fullness.

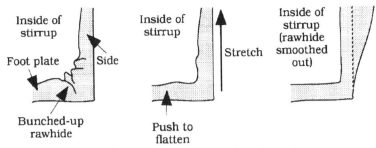

Inside of stirrup

Foot plate — Side

Bunched-up rawhide

Inside of stirrup

Stretch

Push to flatten

Inside of stirrup (rawhide smoothed out)

Because of the stretching and the smaller size of the sides, there is now excess rawhide on the sides of the stirrup. Pull the edges of the rawhide together, keeping them taut and the seams centered, and *carefully* trim off the excess, a little at a time, until you have a 3/8-inch gap as you did on the bottom. Trim in small increments, working the rawhide on both sides to make sure the bunching-up doesn't recur.

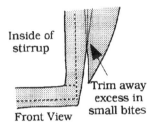

Inside of stirrup

Trim away excess in small bites

Front View

Stitch the side seams together as before, trimming where necessary. It is wise to cut no more than 1/16 of an inch at a time. You can always cut some more, but it's very hard to glue a piece back together. *And never cut the rawhide to fit – stretch it until it does fit.* Keep stretching and pushing to ensure the rawhide stays flat and taut opposite where you've stitched. There will be a tendency for another bunched-up place after the rawhide goes over the top of the sides and meets the bow. Keep it stretched and worked out as you sew.

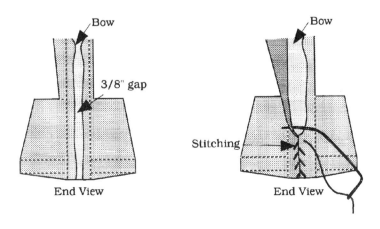

Bow

3/8" gap

End View

Bow

Stitching

End View

It may help to cut some off of both sides of the remaining rawhide. Work any bunched-up area out as before, stretching by pulling, especially on the outside corners. The outside curve of the bow is larger in circumference than the inside curve; stretching the sides of the strips will lengthen them to accommodate this.

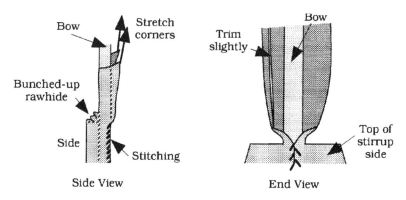

Wrap the rawhide around the bow. Stretch and trim as needed to keep the rawhide taut and flat. The gap between the edges should be about 3/16 inch going up the bow. When you reach the halfway point at the top of the bow, stop on that side and complete the other side the same way.

Trim the ends of the rawhide to abut. Using small stitches, secure the two ends together at the top of the bow.

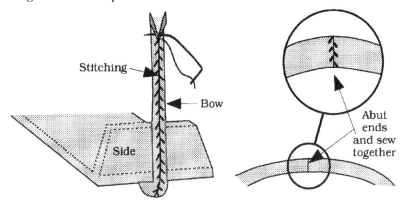

FINISHING THE STIRRUP

While the rawhide is still pliable, use a block as a backer and hammer-tap around the mating surfaces to flatten the seams into form-fitting shape.

Let the stirrup dry thoroughly. The rawhide will shrink to fit tightly as it dries. Working the rawhide breaks down the fibers and gives it "loft" and often a suede-like surface. Remove the suede with some medium-grit sandpaper. Apply a protective coating of shellac, beeswax, or hide glue.

You're done!

HOME TANNING SMALL HIDES FOR FUR

HOME TANNING SMALL HIDES FOR FUR

Doing your own tanning involves work. There are several ways to tan your skins, some requiring more work than others. In general, the more work a tanning method takes, the better job it does.

There is nothing mystical or magical about home tanning. It requires some knowledge of formulas and methods and a few simple tools. (If a Stone Age Indian woman working with primitive implements could tan hides ranging from rabbits to buffaloes, so can you.)

These directions stick to the essentials. Therefore if a tool is recommended, but you want to substitute something you already have, go ahead. It may be better and is considerably cheaper. Switching chemicals or steps in a process sequence is *not* good policy unless you're willing to lose hides as a result of your experimentation.

TOOLS AND EQUIPMENT

To begin your tanning venture, you should have proper, or at least functional, tools and equipment.

You will need to soak the skins. *Never use chlorinated water in any process.* It would be nice to have wooden, earthenware, or enameled barrels and buckets, but those are hard to find and expensive. Plastic or, as a last resort, metal containers which are coated with a rubberized paint (such as Hyperlon) work fine. *Never use bare iron, aluminum, or galvanized containers.* If necessary, a barrel can be lined with a plastic garbage bag. Just be careful it doesn't get punctured or torn. The size of the container will depend on the size and number of skins you want to do. You need a container large enough for the skins to hang or lie in without crowding, but not so large as to waste tanning solution.

A fleshing knife designed for scraping off hair, fat, and excess tissue may be bought or made economically from a piece of power hacksaw blade (often free from a local metal or machine shop), a piece of spring steel, etc. Rivet or bolt a wooden handle on each end or across the top. An old draw knife ("draw-shave") works well, so does a piece of scythe. Even an old butcher knife will do. What you want is a scraping tool that satisfies *you*.

You'll also want a good skinning knife. Your own preference will again rule. A knife with a rounded end usually works best, but a butcher knife or even your own pocketknife will get the job done.

Here is a little trick to cut down on the work of skinning your animals (the fresher the carcass, the better this works). Attach a large hypodermic needle (or even a basketball needle) to a bicycle pump or compressor hose and insert it just under the skin at about the elbow, starting with the rear legs. Blow in air and, with practice, you'll feel the skin just rippling loose over the whole body. The only places you should need your knife will be around the fatty tissue at the top of the rump and around the neck, face, and genitals. Rib meat will not adhere to the hide and you reduce the amount of scraping you have to do later.

For scraping the hide, you may want to use a tanner's beam and/or a frame. For flat hides, a frame can be made from 2x4s or willow limbs bent in a circle.

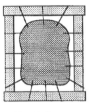
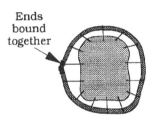

Ends
bound
together

2 x 4 frame   Willow frame

A tanner's beam is simply a log with the bark peeled off that provides a rounded, smooth surface on which to work. The log should be long enough for your hides. You can substitute a 2-inch x 12-inch board, a large-diameter plastic pipe, or even a flat workbench surface.

For a pelt that has been stripped off whole in a "tube" shape (not cut up the center so it will lie flat), you need a stretcher. You can purchase a wire-frame stretcher designed to fit inside the tubed pelt. You also can cut a 1/2-inch- to 1-inch-thick board to shape, square on one end and "V"-shaped on the other. Insert it inside the tubed pelt to stretch it out, the "V"-shaped end fitting snugly into the head. A narrow, preferably triangular, stick called a "shiv" is slipped down the middle on each side of the board to stretch the hide taut and allow circulation of air. A board stretcher is effective and cheap and does a superior job to the more expensive wire frames, especially when it's time for scraping on the hides.

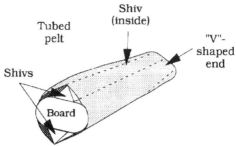

For softening the leather, you'll need a smooth, hard, rounded surface to pull the skin over. A tanner's stake is handy and less tiring to use than the edge of a 2x4, workbench, or car bumper. You can make a good one from a 1-inch x 8-inch or 1-inch x 10-inch board. The length will depend on whether you're going to sit or stand while you work the leather, so adjust it accordingly. Trim one end to a wedge and round off the corners. Sand the whole thing smooth so that the hide doesn't tear or scratch when you work it. It may be built on a base and braced, held in a vise clamped to a workbench, or simply driven into the ground. It's a good idea to have one for sitting and one for standing while you work.

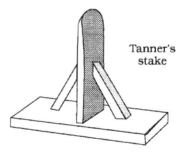

Tanner's stake

There are incidental tools that are useful, such as sandpaper and a block to smooth leather surfaces after tanning and rubber gloves to protect your hands from caustic chemicals. You'll save much time by getting a clothes dryer whose heating element is shot. Often a dryer can be obtained for free and is of inestimable value for drying, softening, and cleaning hides and furs.

A last item – like a lot of this stuff, not absolutely necessary, but very, very handy – is a hand-operated wringer off an old wringer washer. It's excellent for soaking, rinsing, and wringing out skins.

GENERAL INFORMATION

There are several methods of tanning, but essentially the tanning process means:

1. Skinning the animal
2. Stretching the hide and scraping all the meat and fat from the flesh side
3. Washing the hide and scrubbing the last remaining debris from the flesh side

4. Stretching the hide again (to break down the fibers) until it is damp-dry
5. If you want to work with the hide later, salting it to preserve it until you're ready, or
6. Fleshing and tanning the hide, rinsing it, stretching it again, and softening the skin
7. Cleaning and finishing it
8. In some processes as a last step you submit the hide to smoke to make it tough, close the pores for water-proofing, color it, and in general make it usable

PREPARING THE HIDE

Once you have an animal skinned, you'll need to protect the pelt. If you're working with a tubed pelt, leave the hair side inside and insert a drying frame – a wire frame you have purchased or a wooden one you have made. If you use a wooden one, insert a shiv down the center of each side to keep the skin tight and to allow air circulation. As the skin stretches, you may need to increase the size of the shiv to keep the pelt stretched tight – not strained, just firm. The reason for all this is to keep the skin from curling and shriveling as it cools.

If the skin you're working with is cut to lie flat, you can lay it out (skin side up) on a board or piece of plywood large enough to hold it. Large skins may be put on a wall, barn door, or whatever you have that will work. Starting at the middle of one side, work toward both ends, alternately using small brads or nails. Once one side is complete, do the other keeping the nails exactly opposite those on the first side and stretching the hide. Push each tack through the hide first, then drive it into the wood. Be sure the hide is taut with no wrinkles or "loose" spots.

If you use a frame, punch equally spaced holes around the edges of the hide and stretch it out tightly and evenly by lacing cord or rawhide through the holes and around the frame. As with the board, start in the middle and work to both ends, one side at a time.

Once the hide is cooled, it needs to be cleaned. Scrape off as much of the fat, dirt, blood, and other debris as you can. Use the blunt edge of your scraping tool, a blunt knife, or the edge of a kitchen spoon. *Use only blunt edges and be careful not to cut or gouge the skin.* Small, firmly attached pieces that are extremely difficult to remove may be ignored. A later soaking will loosen them.

Remove the skin from its board or frame and weigh it. Complete the cleaning process by washing the hide in warm, soapy water. Remove blood and dirt by scrubbing the flesh side with a stiff brush. Rinse the pelt in clear warm water, wring it out, and put it back on the board or frame to dry. *Be sure to protect it from direct sunlight or heat.*

Some folks like to wait to tan a hide until they have several skins to do at once. If you want to store the hide for a while before tanning, it must be prepared for storage. So when the hide becomes damp-dry, either preserve it as below, or proceed to Fleshing the Hide.

Pour out 1 pound of salt for each pound of hide. Small skins figure out to 2 cups of salt to a pound, so a 1/4-pound skin requires 1/2 cup of salt. Rub in the salt, starting at the middle and working out to the edges. *Cover all of the skin, but be careful not to get any on the hair side.* When all the salt is rubbed in, fold the skin in half, flesh sides together. Roll it up and place it in such a position that the salt solution can drain out of the bundle. Tubed hides, once salted, have to be turned fur side *out* before rolling up. After 36 hours, unroll the skin, shake out the old salt and resalt it, again using the same proportions. Roll the pelt up as before and set it up to drain again. After 48 more hours, put it back in the frame or on the board. For tubed pelts, after the last salting operation has drained, turn it hair side *in* for board-drying (don't forget to insert the shiv). Let the hide dry in a cool, shady spot. A basement, barn, or garage will do.

The hide is now ready for storing until you want to begin the tanning process. Store your hides in a cool, dry place. Skins dried completely for storing will withstand temperature extremes, but the fur tends to deteriorate with extremes of heat or cold. A dried skin stores indefinitely but must be soaked in clear water until it has softened before it can be handled or worked. Moist, salted skins store well for three to five months.

FLESHING THE HIDE

When you are ready to tan the hide, you next prepare a soaking solution by mixing 1 ounce of borax for each gallon of warm soft water. If you have salted hides, scrape off as much salt as you can. Soak the hides in the borax solution until the flesh, tissue, and any remaining debris have loosened, but *in no case for more than 8 hours if you want to save the fur.* An agitator washing machine will save you time and labor and does a better job than you can do by hand. And speed is good because it avoids over-soaking and consequent loosening of the hair. If you use a barrel or pan, stir the hides in solution occasionally. Remember — 4 to 8 hours is sufficient.

When the flesh and fat are loose, lay the hide on your tanner's beam or workbench, flesh side up. With your fleshing tool, scrape away any remaining flesh and debris, especially the tight layer of membrane which completely covers the flesh side of the hide. Unless the membrane is removed, it will wrinkle and tighten to form a hard, crusty layer that most tanning solutions will not penetrate.

Don't rush the scraping process. Use long, regular strokes. Apply pressure, but not so much that you gouge or cut the skin. Scraping takes quite a bit of time and lots of determination, but your effort here has a great effect on the success or failure of your final product. Scraping not only removes undesirable material, it also works the hide to help soften it. When you have finished, all the membranous tissue will have been removed and the flesh side of the hide will be clean, soft, and pliable.

TANNING THE HIDE

Before getting to the tanning formulas, you should know how to tell when a hide is tanned sufficiently. When the hide has soaked in the tanning solution for the minimum time specified, cut a small piece from the edge and look at it. If the piece shows the same color all the way through the thickness without a lighter strip in the middle, it is done. If you want to be absolutely sure, drop the piece in some boiling water for five minutes. If it curls up and hardens, it's not done. If it gets rubbery and curls a bit, tan it some more and test again in a couple of days.

All chemicals must be rinsed from the hide at the rinse cycle of each step. It is especially critical at the end of the tanning cycle to ensure the chemical action is stopped. Otherwise, the process continues and the hide may be lost.

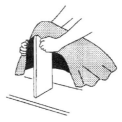

If your hide is not soft when it dries after tanning, you may dampen it again and work it over a tanner's stake until it becomes soft and pliable.

Now you are ready to start the tanning process. Any number of methods and formulas will work. Six are presented here, and you should experiment to find the one that works best for you. The formulas, as written, may not provide enough solution if you are doing several hides or a fairly large one – just increase the amount of solution following the same proportions.

FORMULA 1

A simple method for tanning small skins is to mix together:

    1 gallon of water
    1 ounce of commercial-strength sulfuric acid (battery acid will do)
    1 quart of salt

Soak the hide in this solution for three days. Remove it, rinse it thoroughly, and wring it dry. Then soak it overnight in a solution of:

    1 gallon of water
    1/2 cup washing soda (to neutralize the acid)

Rinse the hide thoroughly again. Wring and stretch it until it's dry and soft. If it is not soft when it dries, dampen it and work it over a tanner's stake.

FORMULA 2

A formula for either small or large skins is to mix:

1 pound of alum
1 gallon of water

In another container, mix:

4 ounces washing soda
1 cup of salt
1/2 gallon warm water

Pour the salt/soda mix *slowly* into the alum mix, stirring while you pour.
Submerge the skin in the mixed solution for 48 hours (small skins), stirring occasionally, or 3 to 4 days for larger skins. Try the tanning test and rinse the skin thoroughly.
Neutralize the tanning solution by rinsing the skin in a mixture of:

1 ounce of borax
1 gallon of water

Soak the hide for at least 1 hour (longer for heavy skins), then rinse in clear water.
Squeeze, don't wring, the water out of the hide and stretch it on your frame or board, flesh side out. Make a solution of:

1 cake Fels Naptha soap
1 cup hot water

While the skin is still damp, put a cooled layer of the soap solution on the flesh side. When the soap has been absorbed, apply a coat of neat's-foot oil to the skin. Be careful not to get any oil on the fur. Re-stretch the skin and place it in a cool spot out of the sun.
When it is damp-dry, rinse the skin thoroughly to clear the soap and chemicals. Squeeze out the water from the final rinse, stretch the skin taut, and put on a coat of neat's-foot oil. Keep it in a cool place out of the sun until it is nearly dry, then work it over a stake until it is soft. The skin may have to be dampened from time to time. Work it until it is soft and supple.

FORMULA 3

Another good small hide formula is to make a paste by mixing:

1 part washing soda
2 parts salt
4 parts alum
Enough water to make a paste

Spread the paste on the flesh side and leave it for 48 to 72 hours. Scrape off the paste and reapply a second coating of new paste. Repeat this process three more times.

Rinse the hide for 10 minutes, stirring and squeezing the hide, in a solution of:

1 pound of borax
1 gallon of water

Rinse the hide in several changes of clear water. Squeeze out the final rinse. When the skin is only damp, stretch it taut and put on a thin layer of neat's-foot oil. When it is nearly dry, work it over a stake until it is supple.

FORMULA 4

A good acid-tanning method is to make a paste of:

1 pound of salt
1/2 ounce sulfuric acid
Enough water to make a paste

Spread the paste over the flesh side of the hide and cover it with a sheet of plastic for 6 hours. Scrape off the paste residue and reapply a new layer of paste, but leave the hide uncovered until the paste dries.

Rinse the hide for 10 minutes in a solution of:

1 pound borax
1 gallon of water

Then rinse the hide in several baths of clear water and squeeze out the final rinse. When the hide is only slightly damp, stretch it taut and apply a light layer of neat's-foot oil. When it has become nearly dry, work it over a tanner's stake to finish it.

FORMULA 5

Yet another small-pelt method is to dissolve:

3 cups salt
2 ounces saltpeter
1 ounce borax
1 gallon of warm water

Add:

1 gallon sour milk
8 ounces sulfuric or battery acid

Mix the solution and put in your hides. Stir every hour for 4 hours. Rinse the hide for 10 minutes in a solution of:

1 pound of borax
1 gallon of water

Rinse the skin thoroughly and squeeze out the final rinse. Stretch it taut while it's damp and apply neat's-foot oil. As it becomes nearly dry, work it over a tanner's stake.

FORMULA 6

This formula works well for pelts up to the size of fox, wolf, and coyote. Wash the fresh hide and let it dry to damp. Being careful not to get any on the fur, rub the flesh side thoroughly with a mixture of:

2 parts salt
1 part saltpeter
1 part alum
1 part baking soda

Fold the skin in half, flesh side in. Fold it in half again. Roll it up tightly, beginning at the middle and rolling outward. Then roll it up in brown paper or newspaper and lay it propped up so that any fluids can drain out. Store it in a cool, dry place for a week or two.

Scrape the skin to remove the mixture and any remaining bits of fat or tissue. Peel off the inside membrane. Place the skin, flesh side up, on a board or frame to dry. As it gets drier, work it over a stake periodically to soften it. By the time the skin is dry, soft, and pliable, it's done. Completely!

CLEANING AND FINISHING THE HIDE

The fur probably looks pretty bad by now. It can, however, be quickly cleaned and groomed.

If it's only slightly dirty, warm some cornmeal, sawdust, oatmeal, bran, or borax in a 250-degree oven for 10 minutes. Spread the meal onto the fur and work it into and over the fur rapidly and vigorously. Shake the meal out and vacuum the fur. Brush the fur in two or three directions to get the rest of the meal out and fluff the fur.

For heavy, stubborn spots, use a commercial cleanser. If it's dirty all over, you can wash it in warm soapy water, then rinse it well and clean as for light soil. The dryer without a heating element comes in handy here. Throw in a pound of sawdust per pound of fur and tumble them for 10 to 15 minutes. Then vacuum and brush the fur.

As a last step, take sandpaper and smooth the flesh side until you're happy with it. Apply a very slight coat of warm neat's-foot oil and let the pelt dry. You're done!

DOWN TO BRASS TACKS: USING TACKS AS DECORATION

DOWN TO BRASS TACKS: USING TACKS AS DECORATION

When early-day traders carried brass tacks to the American Indians, decoration was the natives' first consideration. Many museums display rifle stocks and leather equipment the Indians decorated with tacks of different sizes. Some of those pieces are virtual works of art.

CHOOSING THE TACKS

Decorating such things as belts, pouches, or gun stocks with tacks is not a difficult task, but care and thought must be part of the process. The first thing is to be sure that the tack heads are solid brass, not just brass-plated. Plating wears off quickly and unevenly and – the next thing you know – your beautiful work looks. . .well, *tacky!*

Secondly, get tacks that have steel shanks. Brass shanks can be made to work, but they are unforgiving and can complicate matters.

Tacks come in different sizes and styles – square and round; flat, half-domed, and domed. Which you choose is largely a matter of personal taste, the demands of your design, and the item you decorate. Suppliers' catalogs usually display the types and sizes they sell.

Domed   Half-domed   Flat

PUTTING TACKS IN WOOD

Putting tacks in wood is simple. Just lay out the pattern, choose the appropriate-size tacks, and drive them in. A leather or plastic mallet is kinder to the head of the tack than is a metal hammer.

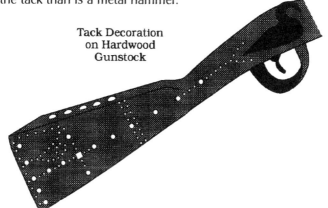

Tack Decoration
on Hardwood
Gunstock

PUTTING TACKS IN LEATHER

Putting tacks in leather is another matter. Unlike wood, leather is supple and soft, and tacks cannot be expected to remain in it for any length of time unless the end of each shank is secured.

There are two commonly-used methods for attaching tacks to leather and each has its adherents. Both systems work but, as with most things, both have strengths and weaknesses. With either system, it is wise to place a lead block with a divot (the size of the tack head) gouged out of it under the tack. This prevents damage to the brass head – dimpling the tack where the shank attaches or even driving the shank right through the cap.

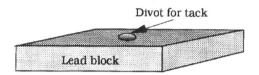

Divot for tack

Lead block

With Method 1, you bend the shank on the underside to secure the tack to the leather. Using Method 2, you push the tack through the leather, then cut the shank and peen it. Peening takes less effort and seems to last longer under use, especially for belts and knife sheaths.

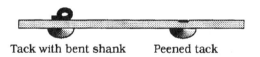

Tack with bent shank   Peened tack

DEVELOPING YOUR PATTERN

Examples of tack patterns may be copied from library books or museum pieces or you may create your own. You may copy any of the examples at the end of this text or use your own creative juices to customize them.

The keys to any good tack decoration are the design and, more importantly, the layout. If you draw a pattern directly onto the leather, even with a pencil, very often the lines will remain on the leather for years. The best method for preventing that is to cut poster board to the same size as your project and make a template.

With pencil, ruler, french curves, or whatever aids you need, lay out on paper the pattern you want. If it is a repetitive pattern, you need only lay out one section and use it over and over. Be very careful in locating the exact spots where the tacks will go; even a small error will show up as a glaring mistake if the tacks are not aligned perfectly on the finished product.

Make holes in the template with a sharply pointed object such as a small round awl. When all the holes are punched, turn the pattern over and, using steel wool, sandpaper, or even your fingernails, remove the "pooched-out" paper so you have a clean hole.

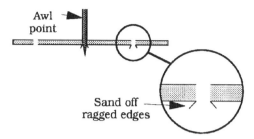

Secure the template to the leather with spring clamps or other tools. Mark the tack placement on the leather. If you used thin poster board, chalk works well and it can be cleaned from the template after use. You can push an awl through the holes into the leather, but this soon enlarges the holes and spoils the pinpoint accuracy required for a truly nice-looking result. If you decide to use an awl, try chalk as well. If the holes close, the chalk will still be there to locate the holes.

If your pattern is repetitive, mark on the leather where the end of the pattern will line up with the next section when you continue.

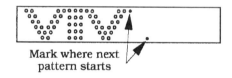

INSERTING THE TACKS

Remove the template and push or drive tacks through the leather, being careful not to "erase" the chalk with your hands. It is extremely important to push the tacks through *straight;* angled tacks do not hold well. A piece of cork or lead under the leather is a big help in catching the tack shanks and preventing damage to your workbench or table. For repetitive work, do one section at a time. If you make holes in the leather and do not insert tacks soon enough, some of the holes are likely to close and you'll have to set up to remark the pattern again.

You can spray dry or over-firm leather lightly with water or alcohol to make it more workable. Don't overdo it. Wipe off excess moisture before tacking.

Method 1: Bending the Shank. Stand the tack, shank up, in a pan. Put the pan in an oven at high heat. Leave it until the shanks turn color.

Remove the pan from the oven and let it cool. The tacks will be malleable enough that they bend easily. Push the tack through the leather. Grip the shank with something like needle-nosed pliers and bend it tightly to the leather. Tap the curled shank lightly to further snug it up.

The discolored brass heads will shine up with brass polish. The polish will clean off the leather with a cloth wet with alcohol or water.

Method 2: Peening the Shank. Once you have a section tacked, turn the leather over and, with a pair of dikes or other tool, cut the shanks flush with the surface. This will require enough downward pressure to ensure no tack shank protrudes above the leather.

You are now ready to peen the tacks. It is wise to practice on a piece of scrap leather before attacking your project. Put a block of lead or other soft, cushioning material beneath each tack as you proceed. Lightly tap each tack shank several times with a hammer. You will notice that the shank shines a little bit as it reshapes into a slightly flattened or "peened over" configuration. The more you strike it, the more chance there is of deforming or damaging the tack head. It doesn't take much force to get the job done, so go easy. The peened shank should just dimple the surface of the leather.

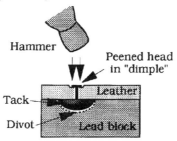

If a tack doesn't peen well or the head breaks, doesn't tighten, or "punches through," carefully remove it. Wet the hole it was in with rubbing alcohol or water and tap the leather lightly with a mallet until the hole closes. Let it dry and reinsert another tack.

With either method, once you've finished the first few tacks, you'll have the "feel" of it. You'll discover that things go much faster than you had expected. Tack decorating becomes fun and very satisfying. It doesn't hurt that tack–decorated leather and wood has a ready market — it is one craft that usually pays well if you want to sell your work!

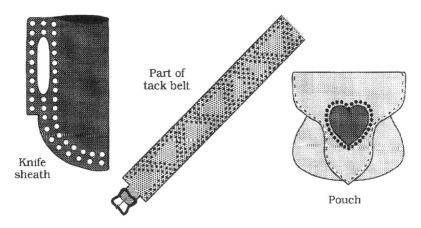

SCRIMSHAW
BASICS

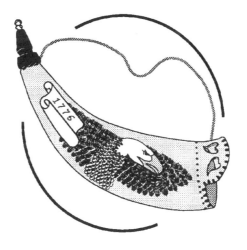

SCRIMSHAW BASICS

Scrimshaw is the art of incising marks that form patterns, pictures, or maps into ivory, horn, antler, or similar materials. It is an old art form that remains popular today.

A practitioner is a scrimshander. Work done by some scrimshanders fetches thousands of dollars. That is understandable because of their evident talent and the fact that the time involved in a given piece can span a year or more.

Ivory is the material of choice among many scrimshanders, but the cost of good ivory can be prohibitive for a novice and some trade restrictions can apply. Scrimshanders also work in other mediums that are affordable alternatives: antler, bone, cow horn and micarta (artificial ivory made from plastic combined, under pressure, with various filler materials).

It is the rare person who can pass by a nicely scrimshawed powder horn. Most people have to stop and examine each example they see. Just because of their beauty, the artistic horns are often purchased by people who have no practical use for them. Even beginners are usually able to sell their work, often opting to do so until they produce a horn that is satisfying enough to keep.

MATERIALS

The tools required for scrimming are pretty basic, although it is possible to squander a lot of money on things that look good (but won't help you much), such as power grinders and etchers. Basically you will need:

Cow horn
Bath-size towel
Wax-free transfer paper (preferred), like that made by Saral
    (inexpensive at most art supply stores), or carbon paper
Tracing paper
Artist's paint brush
Speedball Block Printing oil-based ink (preferred, at art supply
    stores) or india ink
Very fine steel wool
White water-based paint (optional, see p. 147)
Fixative (at art supply stores)
Number 11 needles, and/or
Exacto knife and blades. Two types work especially well:

Cow horns are readily available and reasonably priced. Their shape and grain present challenges that help the novice learn techniques that make scrimming on other materials easier. Beef processing plants and some farmers or ranchers often have horns that they will gladly part with for little or no money. These horns will take more work — they have to be boiled out and cleaned, the walls thinned (without loss of all the outer surface), and imperfections and scratches removed — before scrimming can begin.

There are suppliers who sell cow horns that have already been cleaned and are reasonably priced. Sometimes their horns have been polished. If you prefer a horn that has a flat or dull finish, use fine steel wool to break the polish and achieve that result.

You can, and probably will, develop an elaborate set of tools as you progress. Some people prefer a number 11 needle or a scribe, engraver's tool, or even a pocketknife to an Exacto blade. Others use a sandbag or silly putty instead of a towel for holding the horn while working on it.

Sharp tools are a must for any scrimming. If you buy Exacto blades, get the large package; needles, the same. You *can* sharpen both, but sharpening your own has limitations compared to factory-sharp. The differences make the cost of new tools worthwhile.

Especially for beginners, horns that are white, at least in the area you want to scrimshaw, are best. For your first effort, get one that doesn't have too much curl or taper unless you have the ability to draw your picture freehand directly onto the horn's surface.

You will also need a well-lighted work area. Some people use just the light they have available, but others get one of those round fluorescents with a magnifying glass in it.

BASIC SCRIMSHAW TECHNIQUES

There are probably as many scrimming techniques as there are scrimshanders. To get started, it is good to understand a few basics.

Scrimshaw is not relief carving. It is done by scratching the surface of the material and then putting a coloring agent, such as ink, in the marks. Expert scrimshanders can control the depth and width of their cuts so the inking will produce a work that is blended to produce ship's sails that appear full-bellied or animals with fur that begs to be brushed. Besides talent, that takes practice.

There are essentially two types of cuts: lines (scratches) and stipples (tiny dots).

Fur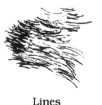

Lines   Stipples

Background

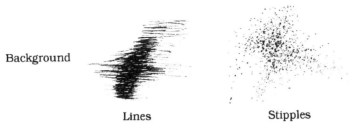

Lines   Stipples

Experience teaches which method works best for a given application. Stippling with a blade point is a tricky venture on horn — horn tends to chip or "blow out" easily. You can stipple with a knife point on some materials, but a scribe or round-point needle works best on horn. You need a larger-tipped needle for horn than for other materials because small holes made in horn tend to close.

There are two types of lines that are especially useful for scrimming on horns: hatching and parallel.

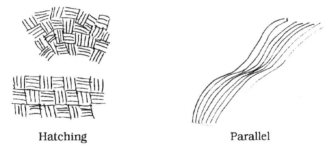

Hatching   Parallel

In rendering these techniques, keep the blade at a 90-degree angle (left to right) so the cuts are not slanted into the horn. Slanted cuts will take the ink oddly and will not look good.

Correct
(90 degrees
left to right)

Incorrect
(not 90 degrees
left to right)

Not only that, angled cuts in horn often result in chipping. And we're not talking massive cuts here. The lines you make are just scratches a couple of thousandths of an inch deep.

PREPARING TO SCRIMSHAW

Finish working out any nicks or sanding marks in the horn with the finest steel wool. If you can draw your pattern or picture freehand, the horn is now ready for you to do so.

Otherwise, find the picture you want. Determine the size it needs to be and reduce it to that size. Your local copy service can do a good job with the reduction feature of their copy machine. Sometimes reducing coarsens the lines of the picture. There are two ways around this problem. Before reduction, use a hard, fine-lead pencil to trace the picture onto some good tracing paper and have that copied. This will eliminate some unwanted detail and keep the copy pretty sharp. You can reverse the process by tracing the reduced copy. In either event, use the best tracing paper you can get.

Transfer the pattern by attaching the paper to the horn and tracing over it. The transfer medium depends on your preference. You may prefer the historical method of making graphite paper (rubbing over the surface of a piece of paper with a soft pencil) and using that like carbon paper. You can use the kind of carbon paper found between sheets of some forms or the kind typists used before the advent of copy machines. Either of these methods works better if, before making the transfer, you first clean the horn with alcohol to remove finger oils and other residues and then coat the horn with a thin layer of white water-based paint.

If historical processes are not important to you, wax-free transfer paper works best. It doesn't smear and resists rubbing off by handling. It can be easily removed with a cloth or tissue dampened with water and doesn't mark up your hands. Even better, it comes in a variety of colors. The red really shows up well when the lighting isn't great. One further benefit is that you can skip the extra work of applying and then getting rid of a coat of paint.

Whatever transfer medium you choose, attach it to the paper pattern. You can use clear tape to bind the edges of the two papers together (transfer medium toward the horn) and to attach the pattern to the horn. This is not a simple matter because the horn tapers in all directions and will make the paper wrinkle.

A better method than tape is to use either a non-drying stick glue or the glue for pool table felt that comes in a spray can. Cover the entire back of the pattern with a *thin* layer of glue and put it on the tracing paper.

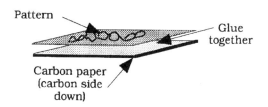

Now cut the pattern in pieces small enough to fit the contours of the horn and attach them with tape. Make sure all the lines of the cut pieces are aligned properly. This way you will avoid a lot of wrinkles.

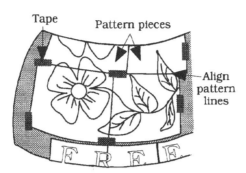

Use a hard-lead drafting pencil with a good, but not sharp, point to trace over the pattern. You don't want to tear the paper. Try not to press the heel of your hand on the paper – if you do, you may pull a piece out of alignment.

When you have finished tracing, carefully remove the pattern pieces and check your work. If there are small sections of line missing, draw them in freehand with a soft-lead pencil. Be careful that you don't touch the transfer if you used homemade graphite paper or carbon paper. The lines will smear and/or disappear. If you didn't use paint, you can make the lines safe by spraying the horn with a fixative or a clear matte spray varnish, but go lightly. Should you object to a protective finish and you used transfer paper, you can dispense with any protection, provided you take reasonable care when handling the horn.

SCRIMSHAWING THE HORN

Now that you have the pattern drawn onto the horn, you are ready to begin scrimming. Use the folded bath towel to steady and cushion your work. Hold the horn with your free hand. Keeping your cutting tool at a 90-degree angle to the horn, begin with the outside of the pattern. Turn the horn as needed to keep the work in front of you and the tool at a right angle. Don't try to make the cut deep. You can go back over it later if a cut isn't deep enough to take the ink the way you want. Move from the outside in until you have completed scratching in all the lines.

It is possible to get quite artistic. A background can be laid in first and then a foreground laid on top of it. Sometimes stippling can be used with lines for a nice effect. Because horn has a tendency to catch the scrimming tool and give it directions you never intended, it sometimes pays to lay in deeper "limit lines" or "stoppers" before scrimming in long detail lines. Lines or stipples that are deeper and closer together will show as darker areas and those that are shallower and farther apart give the impression of lighter tones.

If your pattern has radical or tight curves in it, you may find it difficult to draw them in freehand. Try this simple aid. Cut the side out of a plastic milk bottle. Take a copy of your pattern and trace the curve onto the plastic. Cut it out and use it as a guide on the horn. The plastic is flexible enough to bend to the contours of the horn while maintaining the shape of the pattern curve.

If you want to emphasize part of the drawing by use of heavier lines, get a heavier (wider) tool or make a deeper cut, thereby forcing a wider scratch. Sometimes a single-edged razor blade is just the ticket. But go easy! You don't have to go very deep to achieve what you are after.

Sometimes you will forget to hold the tool firmly enough and end up making an errant scratch that you know is going to catch ink and spoil the effect of your work. Try using a Pink Pearl eraser to rub the scratch out. Or work it out with some very fine sandpaper and then go over it with the eraser. If that doesn't work well enough, use a swab and some rubbing compound.

Scrimming a horn is not a job that has to be done in one sitting. Take your time. The more detailed the project, the more it is going to tire you. Take a break once in a while. If you find your fingers cramping, don't hold the scrimming tool less firmly. Give it a rest! Sometimes you can get relief for your fingers by pushing the tool instead of pulling it. Hey, a scratch is a scratch! Control is the key.

If your vision blurs, get more light or magnification, clean your glasses, or go do something else for a while. This job is not meant to be a marathon, although some people seem to approach it in that frame of mind. If you rush it, you will make egregious mistakes. Take the time to make small cuts that are laid closely together. If you wonder how you are doing during the process, stop and apply some ink to see how it looks.

INKING THE HORN

Buffs of historical accuracy will want to use india ink or concoctions made from black powder or fine wood dust. They all work, but india ink will stick in every pore and give the overall work a grayish hue. Even if you apply the ink to the scrimshaw with a brush, it will cover more than just the lines and stipples. It does not come off with water, although saliva, which contains enzymes, will remove it. India ink comes in a bottle and spills easily. It gets on your fingers and even the finest brushes will touch something that isn't meant to be painted. Spill it on the carpet and see what happens to your marriage!

A wonderful alternative to india ink is Speedball Block Printing oil-based ink. It comes in a tube (doesn't spill) and can be daubed on a cloth, tissue, or brush and applied to your work. The excess wipes off cleanly so it doesn't film or cloud like fast-drying india ink.

Once you've inked your work, examine it to see if you want to rework any parts. When you are satisfied you've done all you're going to do with it, apply a light coat of fixative to the scrimming and you're done. But there is a danger here. Like a certain brand of potato chips, most people find they can't stop with just one!

SUPPLIERS

LEATHER AND RAWHIDE SOURCES

Absaroka Tannery
PO Box 777
Dubois, WY 82513
(305) 455-2440

Spotted Pony Traders
7373 St. Francis St.
Louisville, OH 44641
(330) 875-3064
(800) 875-6553
Winter:
PO Box 68
Hawthorne, FL 32640
(352) 372-4875

LEATHER, TOOLS, TACKS, LACINGS, AND SUPPLIES

The Leather Factory
[For their nearest location and a great catalog, call (877) 532-8437]

Zack White Leather Company
PO Box 315
Ramseur, NC 27316
(800) 633-0396
(One of the most complete tool supply sources and a wide variety of leather and rawhide)

Dixie Gun Works
PO Box 130
Union City, TN 38281
(901) 885-0700
(800) 238-6785
(One of the best catalogues available!)

Crazy Crow
PO Box 847
Pottsboro, TX 75076
(903) 786-2287
(800) 786-6210

Eagle Feather
168 W. 12th
Ogden, UT 84404
(801) 393-3991
(especially needles)

Tandy Leather
(various locations nationwide)

FIRE KIT MATERIALS

Many suppliers offer fire-starting equipment. *Muzzleloader* magazine lists many, so does *The Backwoodsman*. Many mountain man rendezvous have traders who carry strikers. Catalog houses, such as Dixie Gun Works, have a wide array of styles. Often blacksmiths will craft one while you wait.

Muzzleloader Magazine
Rt. 5, Box 347-M
Texarkana, TX 75501-9442

(903) 832-4726
(800) 228-6389 (for subscriptions)

The Backwoodsman
PO Box 627
Westcliffe, CO 81252
(719) 783-9028

Dixie Gun Works
PO Box 130
Union City, TN 38281
(901) 885-0700
(800) 238-6785

KNIVES

Razor Edge Systems
PO Box 150
Ely, MN 55731
(218) 365-6419
(508) 481-5944
(Stones, guides, and a great book on sharpening and tools)

DMT
85 Hayes Memorial Drive
Marlborough, MA 01752
(Diamond hones, rod guide systems)

GATCO
PO Box 600
Getzville, NY 14068-0600
(Rod guide sharpening systems)

GOURDS

There are lots of gourd suppliers, such as:

Little River Gourd Farm
749 Little River 51 N
Foreman, AR 71836
(870) 542-7076

The Caning Shop
926 Gilman Street
Berkeley, CA 94710
(510) 527-5010
(800) 544-3373

A variety of gourd seeds are available at a low price (Native Americans get seeds free) from:

Native Seeds/SEARCH
526 N. 4th Ave.
Tucson, AZ 85705

SCRIMSHAW

You can order clean, polished horns from:

Dixie Gun Works
PO Box 130
Union City, TN 38281
(901) 885-0700
(800) 238-6785

Most other supplies for scrimshawing can be found at your local art supply store.

BIBLIOGRAPHY

FIRE KITS
Numerous outdoor or survival books and articles have been written on fire-starting by nontraditional means. They may be found in your local library or bookstore. *The Book of Buckskinning*, Vols. I and II, cover the subject in detail.

KNIVES
Your local library may have a number of books about knife-sharpening. Some are particularly good:

Juranitch, J. *The Razor Edge Book of Sharpening*. New York, NY: Warner Books, 1985. This is probably the best knife-sharpening book you'll find.

Lee, L. *The Complete Guide to Sharpening*. Newtown, CT: Taunton, 1995.

GOURDS
Information is available from:

Native Seeds/SEARCH
526 N. 4th Ave.
Tucson, AZ 85705

The American Gourd Society, Inc., is a very active organization. Membership is cheap (about $5 per year). The Society publishes a quarterly magazine full of events, tips on all facets of gourding, and want-ads chock-full of suppliers and gourd-related items. It also has pamphlets and handouts available on many aspects of growing and working with gourds.

The American Gourd Society, Inc.
Box 274
Mount Gilead, OH 43338-0274

LAZYBACKS
Laubin, R. and G. *The Indian Tipi: Its History, Construction, and Use*. Norman, OK: University of Oklahoma Press, 1957.

INDEX